3028232

A NEW LOOK AT
ACCOUNTING FOR PENSION COSTS

Pension Research Council

Other Publications of the
PENSION RESEARCH COUNCIL

Concepts of Actuarial Soundness in Pension Plans—*Dorrance C. Bronson*

Social Aspects of Retirement—*Otto Pollak*

Positive Experiences in Retirement—*Otto Pollak*

Ensuring Medical Care for the Aged—*Mortimer Spiegelman*

Legal Protection of Private Pension Expectations—*Edwin W. Patterson*

Legal Status of Employee Benefit Rights under Private Pension Plans—
Benjamin Aaron

Decision and Influence Processes in Private Pension Plans—
James E. McNulty, Jr.

Fulfilling Pension Expectations—*Dan M. McGill*

Collectively Bargained Multi-Employer Pension Plans—*Joseph J. Melone*

Actuarial Aspects of Pension Security—*William F. Marples*

Status of Funding under Private Pension Plans—*Frank L. Griffin, Jr.*
and *Charles L. Trowbridge*

Guaranty Fund for Private Pension Obligations—*Dan M. McGill*

Preservation of Pension Benefit Rights—*Dan M. McGill*

Retirement Systems for Public Employees—*Thomas P. Bleakney*

Employer Guarantee of Pension Benefits—*Dan M. McGill*

Reciprocity among Private Multiemployer Pension Plans—
Maurice E. McDonald

Fundamentals of Private Pensions—*Dan M. McGill*

Pension Mathematics—*Howard E. Winklevoss*

Social Security and Private Pension Plans—*Dan M. McGill* (Editor)

A New Look at Accounting for Pension Costs

WILLIAM D. HALL

and

DAVID L. LANDSITTEL
Partners, Arthur Andersen & Co.

Published for the

Pension Research Council
Wharton School
University of Pennsylvania

by

RICHARD D. IRWIN, INC.   Homewood, Illinois   60430
Irwin-Dorsey Limited   Georgetown, Ontario   L7G 4B3

First Printing, February 1977

ISBN 0-256-01971-1
Library of Congress Catalog Card No. 76–62634
Printed in the United States of America

Bert Seidman, *Director, Department of Social Security*, AFL-CIO, Washington, D.C.

Robert Tilove, *Senior Vice President*, Martin E. Segal Company, New York City

Charles L. Trowbridge, F.S.A., *Senior Vice President*, Bankers Life Company, Des Moines

L. Edwin Wang, *Executive Secretary*, Board of Pensions of Lutheran Church in America, Minneapolis

Howard E. Winklevoss, *Associate Professor of Insurance*, University of Pennsylvania, Philadelphia

Howard Young, F.S.A., *Special Consultant to the President*, United Automobile Workers, Detroit

PURPOSE OF THE COUNCIL

The Pension Research Council was formed in 1952 in response to an urgent need for a better understanding of the private pension mechanism. It is composed of nationally recognized pension experts representing leadership in every phase of private pensions. It sponsors academic research into the problems and issues surrounding the private pension institution and publishes the findings in a series of books and monographs. The studies are conducted by mature scholars drawn from both the academic and business spheres.

Foreword

FOR MORE THAN a quarter of a century there have been sharp differences of opinion within the accounting profession as to the proper treatment of the costs of a pension plan by the sponsoring employer. The first formal attempt to bring some uniformity into the treatment of such costs was made in 1948 with the publication of *Accounting Research Bulletin No. 36* by the Committee on Accounting Procedure of the American Institute of Certified Public Accountants. The pronouncement dealt only with the treatment of past service costs, a perennially troublesome issue, and expressed the view that past service costs should be charged to current and future accounting periods, not to surplus. It did not require that past service costs be recognized for accounting purposes, nor did it contain any guidelines as to how periodic pension costs should be reflected in the income statement of the employer.

With the continued expansion of pension plans and a growing belief on the part of some observers that a pension plan gives rise to substantive ongoing commitments, if not legally enforceable liabilities, the AICPA Committee on Accounting Procedure in 1956 issued another pronouncement on pension costs, *ARB No. 47*. In this Bulletin the Committee expressed a preference for the accrual basis of pension cost accounting, in contrast to the then prevalent practice of charging to pension expense only those sums transferred to an irrevocable pension trust or to an insurance company. The Committee also expressed a preference for charging past service costs over some

reasonable period on a systematic basis. The force of this pronouncement, which was not binding in any event, was weakened by the
Committee's willingness to limit the accrual concept only to the
benefits that had vested—at a time when vesting provisions were far
less liberal than now and in some plans were nonexistent.

Because of the flexibility accorded by *ARB No. 47*, pension accounting practices continued to be divergent, complicating the interpretation of financial statements. This led the Accounting Principles
Board, which had supplanted the Committee on Accounting Procedure in 1959, to commission a comprehensive study of pension cost
accounting. This study was carried out by Ernest L. Hicks, Partner in
Arthur Young and Company, and since 1968 a member of the Pension Research Council. Mr. Hicks' conclusions were published in
Accounting Research Study No. 8, "Accounting for the Cost of Pension Plans," which served as part of the basis for *Opinion No. 8* of
the Accounting Principles Board, issued the following year (1966).
In *Opinion No. 8* the Accounting Principles Board officially endorsed
and prescribed the accrual basis of accounting. Under this opinion
the employer must reflect on his books of account a pension expense
or charge at least equal to the normal cost of the plan plus interest
on the unfunded actuarial liability, and plus a specified additional
amount, when required to reduce the unfunded liability for *vested*
benefits. If any additional amount for vested benefits is required, the
total annual charge need not exceed the normal cost of the plan plus
an amount required to amortize or accrue the initial supplemental
liability over a period of 40 years. The supplemental liability cannot
be accrued at a rate higher than 10 percent per year. The annual cost
accruals can be computed under a range of actuarial cost methods,
each of which produces costs peculiar to its own characteristics, and
great flexibility is permitted in the amortization of supplemental liabilities. There is no requirement to reflect unfunded actuarial liabilities on the balance sheet of the employer, except to the extent that
the required accruals have not been funded, unless the employer has
a "legal obligation" for pension costs.

With the enactment of the Employee Retirement Income Security
Act (ERISA) in 1974, which imposed numerous reporting requirements on pension plans as well as limited legal liability on a plan
sponsor for inadequacy of plan assets upon plan termination, there
has been renewed interest in accounting for pension costs. The Financial Accounting Standards Board which took the place of the

Preface

THE PENSION RESEARCH COUNCIL's decision to authorize a monograph based on a fresh, conceptual look at accounting for pension costs was most timely. We were delighted to undertake the project.

The latest comprehensive and authoritative pronouncement on the subject was *Accounting Principles Board Opinion No. 8*, "Accounting for the Cost of Pension Plans," issued in 1966. Since then, pension plans have become more significant, both in numbers of participants covered and in benefits provided. The U.S. Congress has enacted the milestone Employee Retirement Income Security Act (ERISA) of 1974, the full implications of which cannot yet be measured. Partly in response to these developments, the Financial Accounting Standards Board (FASB), successor to the Accounting Principles Board, has initiated two companion projects, one dealing with accounting and reporting for employee benefit plans and the other with accounting for pension costs. Although a *Discussion Memorandum* has been issued and a public hearing held on the former, the FASB has not yet taken a position with respect to either of these matters. We hope, therefore, that this monograph will assist the Board in its deliberations.

The difficulties of establishing standards governing accounting for pension costs run far deeper than the subject itself. Increasingly in recent years, accountants and others have been questioning the basic framework of generally accepted accounting principles as they exist today. There has been general agreement on the need to identify the objectives of financial statements, and the FASB has established and assigned high priority to a project to accomplish this. As of this writing, however, nothing definitive has emerged. Accordingly, we have considered it necessary to identify, and discuss in considerable detail, the general objectives of financial statements that we believe should be adopted; and we have developed our proposals regarding pension cost accounting in accordance with those objectives.

Recognizing that not all readers will accept our objectives, we have attempted to identify which of our proposals could be adopted within today's accounting framework and which could be implemented only if our overall objectives of financial statements were adopted. We believe our objectives and all of our proposals on accounting for pensions should be accepted, but present adoption of only those proposals that require no change in the basic accounting framework would eliminate many of the deficiencies that exist in today's practice.

We are deeply indebted to many who assisted us during the preparation of this monograph. Although none probably agree with all of our conclusions (and some, we know, have serious reservations), each person with whom we talked or corresponded sharpened our understanding and tested our rationale. In particular, we wish to acknowledge the contribution of Dan M. McGill, chairman of the Pension Research Council; his knowledge, ready availability, and patience greatly aided our efforts. His fellow Council member and associate at The Wharton School, Howard E. Winklevoss, helped by reading an initial draft and offering his candid and penetrating comments. A number of Council members commented on a later draft; and although we did not accept all of their suggestions, the monograph benefited greatly from the reexamination and editing that resulted. And finally, without singling out any by name, we wish to express our appreciation to various of our partners and associates in Arthur Andersen & Co. who either contributed through earlier research on the objectives of financial statements and accounting for pensions or carefully read and commented on our draft manuscripts.

In closing, we shall quote from the letter we sent to the Council members when we distributed a near final draft for their review; it summarizes our approach as follows:

> You will find that we have been innovative in our conclusions and accordingly recognize that readers will not necessarily agree with our views. Although we should like to be sufficiently persuasive

to carry readers along to the same conclusions we have reached, we can hardly expect this in all cases and only hope that our points are presented in a logical, fair, and lucid manner.

January 1977

WILLIAM D. HALL
DAVID L. LANDSITTEL

statement objectives, and their objectives, including a definition of what constitutes an asset and a liability, are set forth at the outset. As might be expected the authors firmly endorsed the concept, legitimatized by *Opinion No. 8*, that the costs of a pension plan should be charged to the accounting period in which they accrue, whether or not they are funded in that period. This, of course, begs the question of when do such costs accrue. As a first step in resolving that issue the authors took the position that the obligation to provide a promised pension benefit to an employee arises when the employee discharges his part of the bargain by performing services for the employer. It follows that the obligation should be recognized and recorded as the services are performed. Since services are rewarded by a wage or salary, which is presumed to reflect the worth of the employee to the firm, the accrual of a pension obligation should be measured in terms of the employee's compensation, irrespective of how the benefit is determined under the terms of the plan.

The second step was to decide how to correlate the emerging pension obligation with employee performance, or its surrogate, compensation. The authors saw two logical ways of doing it, both of which are grounded in actuarial practice and theory. The first would be to assume that the total projected benefit is allocated to the employee's total prospective years of service in such a manner that the resulting *cost accruals* would constitute a level percentage of compensation. Since the cost of each unit of benefit increases as the employee moves closer to retirement, this method in effect would assign a disproportionate number of benefit units (or dollar amounts) to the earlier years of service in order to hold down the assumed cost of benefits in the later years of service. The second method would be to assign to each year of service that proportion of the total projected benefit which the employee's expected compensation for that year bears to the total expected compensation. In other words, the *benefits* assigned to the various years of service under this method would constitute a level percentage of current compensation, in contrast to the first method under which the *costs* would constitute a level percentage of compensation. This method would result in cost accruals that constitute an increasing percentage of the compensation of an individual employee and, in some instances, the compensation of all covered employees, a result regarded by many others to be undesirable.

AICPA Accounting Principles Board in 1973, has appointed two task forces to grapple with the problem, one to develop principles for the measurement and disclosure of pension costs from the standpoint of the pension plan as a separate accounting entity, and another to do substantially the same thing from the standpoint of the plan sponsor. The FASB has already disseminated and held hearings on a voluminous *Discussion Memorandum* on the accounting aspects of the pension plan itself.

There is a host of complex issues, some technical and others philosophical in nature. Some are subsidiary and implemental to a few fundamental issues. The major issues to which all others are related are: (1) how to determine the amount of pension expense to be charged to the operations of the sponsoring employer for each accounting period; (2) whether the unfunded actuarial liability of a pension plan should be shown as a liability on the balance sheet of the sponsoring employer; (3) how to value plan assets, specifically, whether they should be valued at market, original acquisition cost, or some other basis in between these two values; and (4) whether for symmetry or any other reason pension costs and liabilities should be computed on the same basis and in the same manner for the plan and the sponsoring employer.

In view of its long-term and deeply-felt concern over the security of pension plan benefits and proper recognition of accruing pension costs in both private and public sector pension plans, the Pension Research Council 18 months ago approached Arthur Andersen & Co., one of the "Big Eight" accounting firms, to see whether it would be interested in preparing a monograph that would set forth a coherent, theoretical framework within which the foregoing issues could be considered and possibly resolved in a rational way. The firm responded in the affirmative and assigned to the task William D. Hall and David L. Landsittel, both Partners in the firm and members of its policy making group, Mr. Hall being Managing Director of the firm for Accounting Principles and Auditing Procedures. Hall and Landsittel laid out a detailed timetable for preparation of the monograph, which had to compete for attention with many other domestic and international responsibilities of the authors. They adhered to the schedule almost to the day, a performance guaranteed to gladden the heart of any research director.

The authors believe that final resolution of the complex pension accounting issues must be predicated upon a foundation of financial

The authors opted in favor of the second approach despite its unfavorable or unsettling impact on the employer's income statement. They recognized that an employer can have realistic actuarial liabilities for service accrued to date or level annual cost accruals, but not both, since level annual cost accruals produce an actuarial liability in excess of the actuarial value of benefits actually earned to date of valuation. In effect, their decision derived from a conviction that it is more important that the employer's balance sheet reflect realistic values than that the income statement be insulated against fluctuating, but presumably realistic, pension cost accruals. Proration of the total projected benefit by years of service, which would assign equal dollar amounts of benefits to each year of expected service, would generate a more level pattern of cost accruals and a reasonably satisfactory measure of actuarial liability. This approach was rejected by the authors because it is inconsistent with their concept of associating benefit accruals with compensation.

Hall and Landsittel concluded that the unfunded actuarial liability for benefits accrued to date under a defined benefit plan should be shown as a liability on the employer's balance sheet. For accounting purposes it must be assumed that the pension plan will continue indefinitely and that the benefits promised thereunder will ultimately be paid, constituting a claim on the economic resources of the employer. The authors argue that accountants (and others) must look to the substance rather than the form of the pension agreement, ignoring the usual provision that attempts to limit the employer's *legal* obligation to monies already paid to the plan. This provision is operative only if the plan terminates and the authors' premise is that the plan is not going to terminate. For the time being—that is, so long as present accounting rules and conventions prevail, especially the concept of matching expenses and revenues—the authors would offset the liability for unfunded benefits with an asset labeled "Deferred Charges." This asset would be amortized over the remaining period of service of present employees. This would mean that the employer's surplus would not be diminished by reflecting the unfunded pension obligations in the balance sheet. Ultimately, if certain fundamental changes were to be made in the income statement, as recommended by Hall and Landsittel in their initial discussion of their financial statement objectives, any increase in unfunded liabilities, whatever the source, would be charged to expense in the accounting period in which the increase takes place. This would, of course, eliminate the need for the questionable asset "Deferred Charges."

Perhaps the most controversial conclusion of the authors is that pension plan assets should be carried at market value for accounting purposes, since the balance sheet purports to present a "snapshot" picture of the firm's resources and liabilities at one point in time, unaffected by judgments as to future events. They recognize the validity of the argument that under such a rule the valuation of pension liabilities should also reflect market considerations. In their view, this correlation of market values could be accomplished by periodic changes in the rate of investment return assumed in the calculation of pension liabilities, the adjustments stopping short of "fine-tuning." They also concede that an employer's funding policies may properly be based on different principles than those underlying accounting practices. In particular, it may be desirable to smooth asset market values in some fashion for funding purposes.

Finally, the authors believe that there should be symmetry between the pension plan and the employer in accounting for pension costs and liabilities. They buttress their position by arguing that a pension plan has no economic substance apart from that of the employer. The plan is merely a vehicle for discharging the obligation undertaken by an employer in promising a set of pension and related benefits. In their view, the obligation to provide pension benefits cannot logically be considered a liability of the plan unless it is first considered a liability of the sponsoring employer. It is the employees' services to the employer that provide the basis for recognizing and measuring the liability for pension benefits.

All in all, Hall and Landsittel have produced a monograph that is a model in clarity, coherence, and internal consistency. They have met the challenge of providing a framework of accounting theory and principles within which to debate and perhaps resolve the complex issues confronting the accounting and actuarial profession in the pension sector. Their premises, reasoning, and conclusions will not be accepted by all of their fellow accountants nor by all actuaries and corporate financial officers. As a matter of fact, the monograph has generated a number of dissenting statements by members of the Pension Research Council, the statements appearing in the Appendix of this volume. Other members who did not prepare formal statements disagree in varying degrees with some of the authors' conclusions. Nevertheless, the monograph should admirably serve the purpose for which it was intended. Hall and Landsittel have earned the admiration and gratitude of all concerned with the resolution of this critically important issue.

January 1977   DAN M. McGILL

Contents

chapter 1

Introduction

LONG-TERM CHANGES in social and economic conditions have resulted in a continuing change in the nature of pension benefits and an increase in their significance to business enterprises in the United States. Prior to World War II, many pension arrangements were informal in nature, with payments made by employers on a discretionary and sometimes sporadic basis. Since that time, however, the adoption of more formal pension plans has become increasingly widespread. The employers' cost of providing pension benefits has increased dramatically until it presently constitutes a significant portion of total employee compensation costs. As these changes have developed, it has become increasingly evident that a business enterprise undertaking a pension plan incurs a substantive ongoing obligation. The enactment of The Employee Retirement Income Security Act of 1974 (ERISA), with its standards for vesting and funding, provides additional evidence regarding the substantive ongoing nature of today's pension obligation.

The evolution of accounting standards that properly communicate the economic substance of pension-related transactions has not kept pace with these changing conditions. Although *Accounting Principles Board* (APB) *Opinion No. 8*, "Accounting for the Cost of Pension Plans," was indeed a significant forward step when it was issued ten years ago, the accounting rules provided by that *Opinion* are no longer adequate.[1] The principal deficiencies with respect to pension cost accounting that we see today are as follows:

---

[1] American Institute of Certified Public Accountants, "Accounting for the Cost of Pension Plans," *APB Opinion No. 8* (New York, 1966).

1

1. Equally acceptable actuarial cost methods result in widely differing patterns of cost recognition allowable as a means of accounting for similar economic circumstances. Differing methods available for the amortization of unfunded past service costs compound this problem.
2. The unfunded obligation for accrued pension benefits is not recognized as a liability.
3. Varying spreading and amortization techniques result in the artificial leveling of pension expense even in cases where the economic facts are to the contrary.
4. There is too great a latitude in the application of actuarial assumptions.

Clearly, accounting for the cost of pension plans is complex and involves many interrelated issues. The Financial Accounting Standards Board (FASB) has issued a comprehensive, detailed *Discussion Memorandum*[2] and held a public hearing with respect to the accounting by pension plans as separate reporting entities. In addition, the FASB has undertaken a companion project, "Accounting for the Cost of Pension Plans," regarding the measurement of the costs of pension benefits provided by the sponsoring employers.

THE NEED FOR FINANCIAL STATEMENT OBJECTIVES

One of the major reasons why accounting standards have failed to keep pace with the changing nature and significance of pension benefits is that accountants have not agreed on the objectives of financial statements. Since we are unable to formulate and discuss meaningful accounting standards for pension costs absent such objectives, we have found it necessary in this monograph to identify and use those objectives of financial statements that we believe should apply.[3]

As will be discussed in Chapter 3, we believe that the overall pur-

---

[2] Financial Accounting Standards Board, "An Analysis of Issues Related to Accounting and Reporting for Employee Benefit Plans," *Discussion Memorandum* (Stamford, Connecticut, 1975).

[3] Although most of our recommendations for changes in the manner of accounting for pension costs could be implemented within the general framework of accounting that exists today, we recognize that one of our principal proposals would probably require a change in basic concepts. We identify that proposal and suggest an alternative approach (interim, we would hope) that would go a considerable way toward meeting our objectives but that could be applied under today's general standards.

pose of financial statements is to communicate information concerning the nature and value of the economic resources of an entity as of a specified date, the interests of various parties in such resources as of that date and the changes in the nature and value of those resources from period to period. Only when such information with respect to the value of economic resources is properly communicated can users of financial statements effectively rely on those statements as a basis for making their economic decisions. These economic decisions are forward looking, and the financial statements must communicate the value of the enterprise's resources and the past changes in these values in a manner that will be most helpful to the users in their assessment of the future.

One outgrowth of our objectives is a requirement that, for an economic resource to qualify for recognition as an asset in a balance sheet, it must possess the three characteristics of utility, scarcity and exchangeability. Exchangeability means that an economic resource is separable from the business as a whole and has value in and of itself. Intangible assets and deferred charges do not meet this criterion and, consequently, should be excluded from the balance sheet of a business enterprise.

ACCOUNTING FOR PENSION PLANS

In Chapter 5, we shall describe an overview of the standards we advocate for adoption with respect to the accounting for pension plans as separate reporting entities. Our conclusions in this regard are consistent with our financial statement objectives. Although we believe that these conclusions are also consistent with generally accepted accounting principles as they exist today, the FASB has not yet issued an accounting standard based on the *Discussion Memorandum* and public hearing referred to earlier in this chapter; and, in the absence of such a standard, present practice regarding the accounting for pension plans as separate reporting entities is diverse in many respects.

The various classes of assets of a plan should be accounted for using current value as a measurement basis. Information about the value of the plan's economic resources is consistent with the needs of the financial statement users—that is, such information is relevant to (a) an evaluation of the extent to which employees' rights to pension benefits are secure, (b) an evaluation of earnings perform-

ance of the plan's assets and (c) an evaluation by the employer of
the adequacy of funding. Historical asset cost has no particular relationship to a plan's ability to meet its obligations for present and
future benefits, nor to any evaluation of earnings performance or
plan security.

Similarly, our objectives are best met by recording in the plan's
financial statements some measure of the obligation for pension benefits. Information with respect to this obligation is meaningful to
financial statement users in their evaluations set forth in the preceding paragraph. This obligation for plan benefits should be recorded
in employee benefit plan financial statements as such benefits are
earned by the employees—that is, as the employees' performance,
measured by service rendered to date, has been completed. Stated
briefly, our view is that the recording of such pension obligation
should be correlated with direct compensation cost, using an actuarial
present-value approach. Chapter 6 contains a detailed description
(including illustrative examples) setting forth alternative methods of
correlating the pension obligation with compensation costs, and contains our conclusions regarding the approach that best measures the
obligation for benefits earned to date.

Frequently, a portion of the employee service that enters into the
determination of pension benefits estimated ultimately to be payable
has already been rendered at the time a plan is adopted or amended
to increase benefits. An obligation exists at the time of such adoption or amendment based upon this service already rendered, and
the related liability should immediately be recorded.

The measurement of a pension obligation, whether made in accordance with the criteria we advocate or by using any other concept, is a complex matter that requires actuarial expertise. Because
we do not possess that expertise, we have limited our discussion in
this monograph to the accounting concept that we believe is appropriate, and have intentionally not suggested the actuarial techniques
or methods that should be followed in achieving the results under
that concept. These techniques might even differ from plan to plan.

ACCOUNTING FOR PENSION COSTS BY THE EMPLOYER

The principles that now govern accounting for pension costs by
the employer are set forth in *APB Opinion No. 8.* Although the approach that we recommend differs from *Opinion No. 8* in many

important respects, we believe that the FASB could issue a financial accounting standard on accounting for pension costs that would incorporate most of our basic proposals without changing the general framework of present accounting practices. This is generally true even if the standard that the FASB issues with respect to accounting for pension plans as separate reporting entities should differ in certain respects from our recommendations. As we shall point out, however, action on one of our recommendations would probably have to be deferred until such time as financial statement objectives along the general lines we advocate are accepted.

If our views on the accounting for pension plans are accepted, we believe that symmetry between the accounting for pension benefits followed by the plan as a separate reporting entity and that followed by the employer in recognizing the costs of the related pension obligations is essential. Looking through the form to the economic substance of pension plan arrangements, we conclude in Chapter 7 that the obligation for pension benefits must logically be considered a liability of the sponsoring employer as well as a liability of the plan. The plan is merely a vehicle for discharging the responsibilities an employer has undertaken to provide pension benefits to its employees. It is the employees' services *to the employer* that provide the basis for recognizing and measuring the plan's liability for pension benefits.

The adoption of the above philosophy on employer/plan symmetry, when coupled with (*a*) our financial statement objectives and (*b*) our conclusions with respect to the proper accounting by a pension plan as a separate reporting entity, leads us to the following conclusions with respect to the accounting for pension costs (under a defined benefit plan) by the sponsoring employer:

1. A liability representing the obligation for pension benefits earned to date, as determined and set forth in the plan's financial statements, should be recorded in the financial statements of the sponsoring employer to the extent that it has not yet been funded.
2. Under existing accounting conventions, the debit that arises when the portion of the liability that relates to past service is recorded would initially be reflected as a deferred charge and amortized into income over the anticipated remaining service of present employees. If our previously noted concept of financial

statement objectives were to be adopted, however, a deferred charge would not be recognized as an economic resource (i.e., an asset) of a business enterprise. Accordingly, the appropriate manner of accounting for that portion of the pension benefits earned by participating employees by virtue of their past service would be to recognize such costs in the financial statements of the sponsoring employer by an immediate charge to income at the time a pension plan is adopted or amended. Such an initial charge should be set forth separately from operating income, using the income statement format set forth in Chapter 7.

3. The effect of actuarial gains and losses on the liability for unfunded pension benefits earned to date should be reflected in the financial statements of the sponsoring employer on a current basis. With respect to that portion of the actuarial gains and losses that represents gains or losses on pension fund investments over and above those assumed as part of the actuarial interest rate assumption, the current adjustment in the financial statements of the sponsoring employer should be separately identified under the income statement caption, "Nonoperating holding gains or losses."

4. The condensed financial position of a single-employer pension plan (developed by following the accounting we have recommended in Chapters 5 and 6) should be disclosed in the notes to the financial statements of the sponsoring employer since the employer bears the risk of ownership of the plan's funded assets. Full consolidation of the assets and liabilities of the plan into the financial statements of the sponsoring employer is inappropriate since the funded assets of the plan are restricted and not available to satisfy the general claims of the creditors of the employer.

If our proposals were to be adopted, we believe that investors and other financial statement users would benefit. Equally accepted alternatives now existing under generally accepted accounting principles would be eliminated. The economic resources of an enterprise and the interests of the various parties in such resources as of a specified date would be reflected in a proper manner, and the changes in such resources would be recorded in the periods in which they occur.

chapter 2

Evolution of Present Practice

ALTHOUGH pension payments have been made by employers to their employees, at least to a limited extent, for more than a century, such payments did not begin to assume their present significance until after the end of World War II. Prior to that time, many pension arrangements were informal in nature with the more formalized plans found only in larger or rate-regulated companies and in governmental units.

In these earlier periods, the costs of pensions were accounted for almost entirely on a "pay-as-you-go" basis—that is, such pension costs were charged to income only as cash payments were made. For the less formalized plans, this practice was consistent with the nature of the arrangement since payments were discretionary and sporadic, and did not even implicitly result in a long-term commitment. For the more formalized plans, this practice was defended on the grounds that (a) the plans were voluntary and could be terminated at any time and (b) any computation of an actuarial liability was subject to too much variation to be meaningful.

Even in these pre-World War II years, however, there was concern because the "pay-as-you-go" accounting method resulted in substantial increases in income statement charges on a year-to-year basis as the benefits increased. In addition, there was concern that such an accounting method resulted in a charge of pension costs to income sporadically as payments were made rather than systematically as the related services were performed by the employees.

Partly in response to these concerns, some companies created a "reserve" for the future payment of pensions by a charge against surplus at the inception of the plan. Some charged pension payments against this reserve rather than reflecting such amounts in the income statement. Such a procedure was rationalized under the presumption that pension costs were not operating costs to the business but, rather, were distributions of a portion of the profits of the business.

A variation of the foregoing method was encountered when a "reserve" was created, at the inception of a pension plan, for only that portion of the ultimate pension liability resulting from employees' services rendered prior to the date of inception of the plan (generally known at that time as the "accrued liability for past services"). The provisions creating such reserves were frequently charged directly to earned surplus on the theory that they applied to prior periods. A few corporations, however, recorded such provisions as adjustments to the income account of the year in which the plan was adopted. In still other cases, the accrued liability for past service was recorded, with an offsetting debit reflected as a deferred charge and amortized through the income accounts in succeeding years.

It is interesting to note that at least some regulatory authorities during this period refused to allow past-service costs as current operating expenses for rate purposes. A Federal Communications Commission report applicable to the Bell System contained the following comments in support for the disallowance of such costs:

> The Uniform System of Accounts . . . recognizes as a proper current cost of telephone service the costs of pensions, for which a bona fide liability to employees exists, that accrue ordinarily through the process of normal contributions. But, the current cost of telephone service cannot be construed from an accounting standpoint to include any portion of the normal current accruals attributable to past years, to be picked up at the election of the utility as a part of the present cost of furnishing telephone service. Such amounts are characterized as past losses to be amortized out of some income or surplus account. The charging of such deferred items or past losses to operating expenses for subsequent years may require rate payers to bear a cost in such years which does not arise out of service rendered to them during those years.[1]

---

[1] Federal Communications Commission, "In the Matter of Additional Charges to Operating Expense Account 672 (Relief and Pensions) in the Uniform System of Accounts for Telephone Companies, Representing four percent of unfunded actuarial liability under the Bell System pension plan proposed by certain wire telephone carriers," *Public Notice 56210, P–21,* Docket No. 5188, Washington, D.C., December 11, 1941.

ACCOUNTING RESEARCH BULLETIN NO. 36

In November 1948, the Committee on Accounting Procedures of the American Institute of Certified Public Accountants (AICPA) issued its first pronouncement dealing with pension costs, *Accounting Research Bulletin* (ARB) *No. 36*, "Pension Plans—Accounting for Annuity Costs Based on Past Services."[2] While *ARB No. 36* recognized that the calculation of past service costs is based on past service, it concluded that such costs "are incurred in contemplation of present and future services, not necessarily of the individual affected but of the organization as a whole." Accordingly, the Committee was of the opinion that:

> (*a*) Costs of annuities based on past service should be allocated to current and future periods; however, if they are not sufficiently material in amount to distort the results of operations in a single period, they may be absorbed in the current year;
>
> (*b*) Costs of annuities based on past service should not be charged to surplus.

ARB No. 36 contained no requirements, however, that past service costs must be recognized for accounting purposes. Neither did it contain any guidelines as to how periodic pension costs should be reflected in the income statement.

ACCOUNTING RESEARCH BULLETIN NO. 47

During the decade after the adoption of *ARB No. 36*, the rapid growth of pension plans resulted in an increase in the significance of pension costs to most business enterprises. It became increasingly evident that a corporation adopting a pension plan does incur a substantive ongoing obligation even if such plans do not give rise to a continuing liability that is legally enforceable. Nevertheless, in those years a great majority of those companies for which information with respect to the accounting for pension plans is available followed the cash basis accounting method. The amount recorded as a pension expense was equal to the amount actually paid out by the employer for pension benefits—either directly to the employees (pay-as-you-go) or through contributions to a pension fund. It should be noted, however, that financial statement disclosure of the method of accounting for pension costs was not common during

---

[2] Subsequently included as Chapter 13A in "Restatement and Revision of Accounting Research Bulletins," *ARB No. 43* (New York, 1953).

these periods; consequently, the prevalence of the various methods is based upon incomplete surveys.[3]

In September 1956, the AICPA Committee on Accounting Procedures again saw fit to deal with pension costs (this time on a broader basis), noting in a new *ARB No. 47*[4] that "[v]ariations in the provisions of pension plans in the United States, in their financial arrangements, and in the circumstances attendant upon their adoption, have resulted in substantial differences in accounting for pension costs." Although acknowledging that some viewed full accrual of pension costs as possibly unnecessary because, among other things, "a company would in all probability never be called upon to utilize the entire amount of an actuarially calculated full accrual," the Committee expressed its preference for the following position:

> In the view of many, the accrual of costs under a pension plan should not necessarily be dependent on the funding arrangements provided for in the plan or governed by a strict legal interpretation of the obligations under the plan. They feel that because of the widespread adoption of pension plans and their importance as part of compensation structures, a provision for cancellation or the existence of a terminal date for a plan should not be the controlling factor in accounting for pension costs, and that for accounting purposes it is reasonable to assume in most cases that a plan, though modified or renewed (because of terminal dates) from time to time, will continue for an indefinite period. According to this view, costs based on current and future services should be systematically accrued during the expected period of active service of covered employees, generally upon the basis of actuarial calculations. . . . Also according to this view, costs based on past services should be charged off over some reasonable period, provided the allocation is made on a systematic and rational basis and does not cause distortion of the operating results in any one year.

The Committee, however, then fell back to a compromise position. It provided that, as a minimum, "the accounts and financial statements should reflect accruals which equal the present worth, actuarially calculated, of pension commitments to employees to the

---

[3] Warde B. Ogden, "Survey of 260 Pension Plans Reveals Wide Variety of Accounting for Costs, Plus Some Hazards," *The Journal of Accountancy*, vol. 93, no. 1 (January 1952) p. 44.

[4] American Institute of Certified Public Accountants, "Accounting for the Costs of Pension Plans," *ARB No. 47* (New York, 1956).

extent that pension rights have vested in the employees, reduced, in the case of the balance sheet, by any accumulated trusted funds or annuity contracts purchased." In the frequent cases where vesting was delayed, this resulted in virtually no minimum accrual requirement.

Because of the flexibility permitted by *ARB No. 47*, accounting for the cost of pension plans continued to vary widely among companies, and on a comparative year-to-year basis within given companies. During 1958, for example, some business enterprises that had previously made substantial accruals for pension costs either eliminated or drastically reduced their accruals. Funds previously provided were more than sufficient to meet the liability for vested benefits, and consequently the requirements of *ARB No. 47* could be met without the additional funding.[5]

In many cases, contributions to pension funds (and the resulting provisions charged against income) varied with fluctuations in company earnings or with the availability of funds. In other instances, pension provisions were affected by their Federal income tax consequences as well as by the extent of recognition of actuarial gains and losses.

A much publicized example (because of its size and visibility, not because it was unique) of the discretionary nature of existing pension accounting practices was the accounting for pension costs followed by the United States Steel Corporation in the years 1957 to 1962. A summary of that company's total provision for pension costs for those years as compared with its income before income taxes is as follows:[6]

	Pension Costs	Income before Income Taxes
1957	$140	$825
1958	33	587
1959	104	488
1960	87	574
1961	85	351
1962	39	296

Note: Dollar amounts in millions.

---

[5] Felix Pomeranz, Gordon P. Ramsey, and Richard M. Steinberg, *Pensions, An Accounting and Management Guide* (New York: The Ronald Press, 1975), p. 85.

[6] United States Steel Corporation, *Annual Reports*, 1957 through 1962.

The decline in U.S. Steel's pension costs charged to income in 1958 resulted from the application of $61 million of contributions, originally provided in prior years for past service costs, to cover the current service costs for the first three quarters of 1958. Consequently, no contribution was funded or charged against income during this nine month period. Fluctuations occurring in other years (most notably in 1962) were due largely to changes in actuarial assumptions and methods of recording actuarial gains.[7] Had the company recorded more comparable provisions for pension costs during these years, the reported net income amounts would have differed significantly.

During these years, many other companies followed pension accounting policies that resulted in equally discretionary provisions. In addition, there were no accounting rules that required financial statement disclosure of either the amount of pension costs charged to income or the method used to arrive at such amount. In U.S. Steel's case, the pension information summarized above was not set forth in financial statement notes but, rather, was included in the letters to shareholders from the Chairman of the Board of Directors, included in the annual reports.[8] For many other companies, no disclosures of this nature were included in any form in their published reports.

ACCOUNTING RESEARCH STUDY NO. 8

As a result of these continuing problems, the Accounting Principles Board (APB) authorized a research study on accounting for the cost of pension plans. The results of this comprehensive, thoughtful study conducted by Ernest L. Hicks were published as *Accounting Research Study (ARS) No. 8*[9] in 1965. ARS No. 8 set the following basic conclusions:

---

[7] Ibid. With respect to the year 1958, the accompanying report of the company's independent public accountants contained two explanatory middle paragraphs fully disclosing the impact of the change in pension funding policies. With respect to 1959, the accompanying auditors' report contained a reference to a section in the Chairman's letter that explained the 1958 and 1959 funding policies. In all years, the amount of pension costs charged to income was equal to the amount of the company contribution to the related pension trust funds, and the auditors' reports contained no qualification with respect to consistency of application of generally accepted accounting principles.

[8] Ibid.

[9] Ernest L. Hicks, "Accounting for the Cost of Pension Plans," *Accounting Research Study No. 8* (New York: American Institute of Certified Public Accountants, Inc., 1965). Copyright 1965 by the American Institute of Certified Public Accountants, Inc.

[T]he actuarial cost methods presently used in calculating payments under pension plans are acceptable for use in accrual accounting if they are applied in accordance with the other conclusions of the study.

[P]rovision should be made annually for the normal cost of a pension plan—the cost assigned, under the actuarial cost method used, to years subsequent to the inception of the plan.

[P]ast service cost should be taken into expense (together with related charges for interest) systematically over a reasonable period following the inception of a pension plan.

[A]n increase in prior service cost, resulting from an amendment of a pension plan increasing benefits, should be taken into expense (together with related charges for interest) systematically over a reasonable period following the effective date of the amendment.

[A]ctuarial gains and losses should in most instances be spread over the current year and future years.

[U]nrealized appreciation or depreciation of common stocks (and, in some instances, bonds and investments of other types) in a pension fund should be recognized systematically in estimating the employer's pension cost for accounting purposes.

[P]resent employees who may reasonably be expected to become participants in a pension plan should be included in calculations of the cost of the plan for accounting purposes.

[I]f the contributions to a pension fund differ from the accounting charges, the latter should include (or be reduced by) interest on the difference between the actual pension fund and a theoretical fund which would have been produced on the basis of the accounting charges.

[T]he unfunded prior service cost of a pension plan is not a liability which must be shown in the balance sheet of an employer. Ordinarily, the amount to be shown for pension cost in the employer's balance sheet is the difference between the amount which has been charged to expense in accordance with the recommendations of this study and the amount which has been paid. If, as may occur in rare instances, participants' vested rights are a liability of the employer, the unfunded present value should appear as a liability; if the employer accounts for the cost of the plan in conformity with the recommendations of this study, the amount should be carried forward as a deferred charge to operations.

[R]outine pension disclosures should not ordinarily be necessary in the financial statements of companies whose accounting for pension cost conforms with the recommendations of the study. If, however, a change in an accounting practice or an accounting change necessitated by altered conditions affects the comparability of the employer's financial statements as between accounting periods, the change and its effect should be disclosed.[10]

In summary, the study recognized the substantive continuing obligation of an employer for pension costs, which obligation overrides the legal terms of a plan allowing for its termination. It recognized that discretionary and inconsistent treatment of actuarial gains and losses was not acceptable. Finally, it confirmed that the provision for pension costs to be recorded should not be dependent upon the manner of *funding* of these costs.

As was the case with other accounting research studies commissioned by the APB, Mr. Hicks' conclusions did not represent authoritative generally accepted accounting principles that were required to be applied in practice.

ACCOUNTING PRINCIPLES BOARD OPINION NO. 8

The next year, 1966, the APB issued its *Opinion No. 8* dealing with the subject of pension costs.[11] Acknowledging the recommendations of ARS No. 8, the Board stated that its "conclusions agree in most respects with, but differ in some from, those in the Research Study."[12] The more significant conclusions of *Opinion No. 8* (included in its entirety as Appendix A to this monograph) are covered in the discussion that follows. As an overview, APB *Opinion No. 8* served to narrow the acceptable alternatives then currently available to business enterprises in accounting for pension costs. Its primary objective was to eliminate the inappropriate fluctuations in pension provisions that existed up to that time.

Costs to Be Recognized on Accrual Basis

Although recognizing that a company may limit its legal obligation to the extent of pension fund assets, the APB noted in *Opinion No. 8* that pension plans generally continue indefinitely so long as the company remains in business. Accordingly, the accounting for pen-

---

[10] Ibid. Chapter 1, "Summary and Conclusions."
[11] AICPA, *APB Opinion No. 8.*
[12] Ibid., paragraph 5.

sion costs should not be discretionary; pension costs should be recognized annually, whether or not funded.

The *Opinion* provided that the entire cost of benefits estimated ultimately to be paid by the sponsoring employer should be charged against income subsequent to the adoption or amendment of a plan. The annual provision should be based upon an accounting method that uses one of the several acceptable actuarial cost methods,[13] with both the accounting and the actuarial cost method consistently applied. The amount of such annual provision should be between the following minimum and maximum:

> Minimum—total of (1) normal cost, (2) an amount equivalent to interest on any unfunded prior service cost and (3) if applicable, a provision for vested benefits. A provision for vested benefits determined in accordance with the *Opinion* should be made if there is an excess of the actuarially computed value of vested benefits (as defined) over the total of (1) the pension fund and (2) any balance-sheet pension accruals, less (3) any balance-sheet pension prepayments or deferred charges existing at the end of the year, provided that such excess is not at least 5 percent less than the comparable excess at the beginning of the year.

> Maximum—total of (1) normal cost, (2) 10 percent of the past service cost, (3) 10 percent of the amounts of any increases or decreases in prior service cost arising on amendments of the plan and (4) interest equivalents on the difference between provisions and amounts funded.[14]

Unfunded Prior Service Cost Not Ordinarily a Liability

APB Opinion No. 8 further concluded that "[t]he difference between the amount that has been charged against income and the amount that has been paid should be shown in the balance sheet as accrued or prepaid pension cost. If the company has a legal obligation for pension cost in excess of amounts paid or accrued, the excess should be shown in the balance sheet as both a liability and a deferred charge. Except to the extent indicated in the preceding sen-

---

[13] These acceptable actuarial methods include an accrued benefit cost method—unit credit method, and four projected benefit cost methods—entry-age normal method, individual-level premium method, aggregate method and attained-age normal method. For a brief description of these methods, see Appendix A of *APB Opinion No. 8.* "Pay-as-you-go" and terminal methods are *not* acceptable under the provisions of *APB Opinion No. 8.*

[14] AICPA, *APB Opinion No. 8,* paragraph 17.

tences of this paragraph, unfunded prior service cost is not a liability which should be shown in the balance sheet."[15]

Actuarial Gains and Losses to Be Spread or Averaged

Opinion No. 8 provides that actuarial gains and losses, including realized investment gains and losses, should be given effect in the provision for pension cost in a consistent manner that reflects the long-range nature of pension costs. In general, the *Opinion* requires that such gains and losses be spread over the current year and future years or recognized on the basis of an average. Unrealized appreciation and depreciation should be recognized in the determination of the provision for pension costs either in the actuarial assumptions or by another rational and systematic basis that avoids giving undue weight to short-term market fluctuations. For example, a five-year averaging technique can be used, and only a portion of any unrealized appreciation (such as 75 percent) need be recognized. Ordinarily appreciation and depreciation need not be recognized for debt securities expected to be held to maturity and redeemed at face value.[16]

Disclosures Required

The *Opinion* calls for the following disclosures:

1. A statement that such plans exist, identifying or describing the employee groups covered.
2. A statement of the company's accounting and funding policies.
3. The provision for pension cost for the period.
4. The excess, if any, of the actuarially computed value of vested benefits over the total of the pension fund and any balance-sheet pension accruals, less any pension prepayments or deferred charges.
5. Nature and effect of significant matters affecting comparability for all periods presented, such as changes in accounting methods (actuarial cost method, amortization of past and prior service cost, treatment of actuarial gains and losses, etc.), changes in circumstances (actuarial assumptions, etc.), or adoption or amendment of a plan.[17]

---

[15] Ibid., paragraph 18.
[16] Ibid., paragraphs 29–32.
[17] Ibid., paragraph 46.

FINANCIAL ACCOUNTING STANDARDS BOARD

Interpretation No. 3

The latest pronouncement with respect to pension cost accounting is a December, 1974, *Interpretation*[18] issued by the FASB, following the enactment of ERISA. In that *Interpretation* (included in this monograph as Supplement B), the FASB concluded that "no change in the minimum and maximum limits for the annual provision for pension cost set forth in . . . *APB Opinion No. 8* is required as a result of the Act." It goes on to note, however, that compliance with ERISA may result in a change in the amount of pension cost to be charged to expense periodically even though no change in accounting methods is made.

In addition, the FASB concluded that ERISA does not create a legal obligation for unfunded pension costs that warrants recognition as a liability pursuant to *APB Opinion No. 8* except under specified (but not common) circumstances.

Discussion Memorandum—"Accounting and Reporting for Employee Benefit Plans"

In October, 1975, the FASB issued a *Discussion Memorandum*, "Accounting and Reporting for Employee Benefit Plans."[19] As with prior FASB discussion memorandums, this one identifies issues and arguments but assumes a neutral stance regarding conclusions.

Although the *Discussion Memorandum* is neutral and addresses itself to the accounting for pension plans, not pension costs (noting that accounting for the two need not be symmetrical), its issuance and comprehensive discussion constitute an important recognition of the importance of pension accounting and provide some insight as to the issues that will affect pension cost accounting. The issues with respect to pension plans identified and discussed in the *Discussion Memorandum* are as follows:

> BASIC ISSUE ONE: What should be the accounting and re-
> porting entity?

---

[18] Financial Accounting Standards Board, "Accounting for the Cost of Pension Plans Subject to the Employee Retirement Income Security Act of 1974," *Interpretation No. 3* (Stamford, Conn., 1974).

[19] FASB, *Discussion Memorandum*.

BASIC ISSUE TWO: What are the unique objectives of financial accounting and reporting for pension plans?

BASIC ISSUE THREE: Which basis of accounting is most appropriate for preparing the financial statements?

BASIC ISSUE FOUR: What measurement basis should be used to account for the various classes of assets of the pension plan?

IMPLEMENTAL ISSUE A: If certain or all plan assets are to be stated in terms of current value, should the FASB prescribe the manner in which that value is to be determined? If so, what approaches ought to be considered?

BASIC ISSUE FIVE: Should some measure of the obligation for pension benefits be presented (a) as a liability or equity interest in the financial statements, (b) as footnote or other disclosure, or (c) not at all?

IMPLEMENTAL ISSUE B: How should the obligation for plan benefits be described or measured?

IMPLEMENTAL ISSUE C: Are present actuarial cost methods and techniques acceptable mechanisms to measure the obligation for plan benefits for purposes of plan financial reporting?

IMPLEMENTAL ISSUE D: If for purposes of plan financial reporting the measure of the obligation for plan benefits is to be based on an actuarial measure, with what degree of specificity should an FASB Statement prescribe the actuarial basis for measuring the obligation?

IMPLEMENTAL ISSUE E: If an obligation for plan benefits is included in a balance sheet presentation, how should any difference between the plan's assets and its liabilities be reported?

BASIC ISSUE SIX: How should the financial activities of the pension plan be reported?

IMPLEMENTAL ISSUE F: If investments are stated in terms of a measurement basis other than historical cost, how should unrealized gains and losses be accounted for?

IMPLEMENTAL ISSUE G: If bonds are stated in terms of a measurement basis other than current value, how should gains and losses on sales be treated in the accounts when replacement purchases of similar investment grade bonds are made?

IMPLEMENTAL ISSUE H: Should the FASB specify how assets and liabilities should be classified in financial statements of the pension plan? If so, how should they be classified?

BASIC ISSUE SEVEN: What disclosures should be required in pension plan financial statements?

BASIC ISSUE EIGHT: Are there any other financial accounting and reporting issues not considered elsewhere in this Discussion Memorandum that warrant special consideration in the accounting and reporting for pension plans?

IMPLEMENTAL ISSUE I: Transitional problems of new accounting and reporting standards for pension plans.

The FASB held a public hearing on this matter in February 1976, but no exposure draft of a Financial Accounting Standard has been issued as of this writing.

Project on Accounting for the Cost of Pension Plans

In addition, the FASB has authorized a companion project on accounting for the cost of pension plans. Although a project task force has been appointed, there has been no announcement of when a discussion memorandum will be issued on this subject. It is possible that the FASB may be deferring any publications or hearings on this subject until action has been taken on accounting and reporting for employee benefit plans.

SEC REQUIREMENTS

The Securities and Exchange Commission has set forth rules and regulations for disclosure of certain pension-related information in notes to financial statements of publicly-held companies in filings with the Commission. These disclosure requirements, which are set forth in Rule 3–16(g) of *Regulation S–X*, parallel those disclosure requirements contained in *APB Opinion No. 8* in every respect except one. An additional requirement of the Commission is that where plans are not fully funded, the amount of unfunded past service costs as of the date most recently determined must be disclosed.

chapter 3

Objectives of Financial Statements

THE NEED FOR OBJECTIVES

An ATTEMPT to develop accounting standards in general or to develop accounting standards dealing specifically with a particular type of entity or transaction cannot ultimately succeed unless that attempt is based on a clearly perceived and broadly accepted set of financial statement objectives.

Obvious as this assertion may seem, it has not generally been recognized, and this lack of recognition lies at the root of many, perhaps most, of the accounting and reporting problems that plague us today. Since financial statements are essentially a means for communicating financial information, the standards for their preparation should be based on the identified needs of users—not on some assumed immutable natural law.[1]

But this is not the case with present accounting standards. Rather than determining how a new type of transaction should be accounted for and reported in relation to an agreed upon objective, accountants have tended to look for the way in which the most similar type of transaction is accounted for and to extend that treatment, by analogy,

---

[1] James F. Strothers notes that "generally accepted accounting principles are not derived from scientific observation of natural law, they are not discovered, but declared." "The Establishment of Generally Accepted Accounting Principles and Generally Accepted Auditing Standards," *Vanderbilt Law Review*, vol. 28, no. 1 (January 1975), p. 203.

to the new transaction. Is it any wonder that the present pattern of accounting is frequently illogical, sometimes even reflecting obvious contradictions, or that it can be defended only by citing arbitrary rules and precedents?

By the time the APB was established over 15 years ago, many accountants and others had come to recognize the need for understood and accepted guidelines and objectives in reaching decisions on specific accounting and reporting problems. Yet, the APB in its 15 years of operations became so embroiled in providing *ad hoc* answers to the ever growing number of emerging problems that it never gave significant attention to the definition of objectives of financial statements. Although the early *Accounting Research Studies Nos. 1 and 3* entitled "The Basic Postulates of Accounting" and "A Tentative Set of Broad Accounting Principles for Business Enterprises" dealt with the subject of financial statement objectives, the APB did not use them as a basis for a pronouncement on objectives. APB *Statement No. 4*, "Basic Concepts and Accounting Principles Underlying Financial Statements of Business Enterprises," issued in 1970, approached the problem backward by attempting to rationalize from existing practice to the concepts and principles, rather than formulating objectives upon which standards for practice could be based; it amounted to nothing more than a codification of existing practices.

It was for this reason and because of increasing public recognition of the need for financial statement objectives that the AICPA created two "blue ribbon" bodies composed of both accountants and others in 1971, one to recommend the manner in which accounting principles should be established and the other to define the objectives of financial statements. The study group that dealt with the manner in which accounting principles should be established, commonly known as the Wheat Committee after its chairman, Francis M. Wheat, issued its report[2] in 1972, which led to the creation of the FASB.

The study group formed to deal with the objectives of financial statements, also called by the name of its chairman, the late Robert M. Trueblood, issued its report[3] in 1973. That report contained

---

[2] American Institute of Certified Public Accountants, "Report of the Study on Establishment of Accounting Principles," *Establishing Financial Accounting Standards* (New York, March 1972).

[3] American Institute of Certified Public Accountants, "Report of the Study Group on the Objectives of Financial Statements," *Objectives of Financial Statements* (New York, October 1973).

a listing of stated objectives accompanied by supporting rationale, but its conclusions have not been adopted. Subsequently developed accounting standards, as formulated by the FASB, have not been predicated upon the Trueblood report's objectives.

The FASB now has a project, "Conceptual Framework for Accounting and Reporting," under way, and it is hoped that the long-awaited identification of financial statement objectives required to deal with specific accounting and reporting problems is not far from reality. At some future date when these objectives have been formulated and adopted, it may prove necessary for us to modify our views regarding accounting and reporting for pension costs. In the meanwhile, we shall identify those objectives of financial statements that we believe should apply, and then use those objectives as the basis for our conclusions and recommendations in the following chapters with respect to the accounting for pension plans and pension costs.

In 1972, the authors' firm issued a book, *Objectives of Financial Statements for Business Enterprises*,[4] that was submitted to the Trueblood Commission during its deliberations. Following this in 1974, the firm issued *Accounting Standards for Business Enterprises Throughout the World*.[5] We subscribe to the objectives and supporting rationale set forth in these books[6] and will draw or summarize extensively from the conclusions contained therein (without detailed annotation regarding source) in the pages that follow.

THE OVERALL PURPOSE OF FINANCIAL STATEMENTS

In our view, *the overall purpose of general-purpose financial statements is to communicate information concerning the nature and value of the economic resources of a business enterprise as of a specified date, the interests of creditors and the equity of owners in the economic resources as of that date, and the changes in the nature and value of those resources from period to period.*

In order that we may (*a*) carefully explain the meaning of the above statement of purpose together with our underlying rationale in support of the statement, and (*b*) fully illustrate how determina-

---

[4] Arthur Andersen & Co., *Objectives of Financial Statements for Business Enterprises* (Chicago, 1972).

[5] Arthur Andersen & Co., *Accounting Standards for Business Enterprises Throughout the World* (Chicago, 1974).

[6] One of the authors was personally involved in certain aspects of their preparation.

tions of the nature of assets, liabilities and income are derived from the statement, we shall discuss the key words and phrases making up this statement in the paragraphs that follow.

Our Definition of "Economic Resources"

We define economic resources as those elements of wealth that possess the three basic characteristics of utility, scarcity and exchangeability and hence have economic value.

The value of an economic resource at any time is the price it commands in exchange. "Exchangeability" as the term is used here is not intended to suggest that an economic resource is necessarily immediately marketable or that it is being held for immediate sale. Rather, exchangeability means that an economic resource is separable from a business as a whole and that it has value in and of itself—that it is not solely dependent on the fortunes of the particular business enterprise to which the resource is attached. In general, the application of the above-described criterion results in the identification of only those elements of wealth capable of securing or satisfying (a) the claims held by creditors or (b) the equities of stockholders, as economic resources to be given recognition as "assets" in the balance sheet.

In addition to its economic resources, a successful business enterprise will generally possess many other elements of wealth that, when employed in conjunction with economic resources, will enhance the capacity of the enterprise to develop additional economic resources. These intangibles, which embrace a range of attributes or favorable circumstances, enable a business enterprise to achieve earnings beyond the pure time cost of money. They reflect the advantages of profit-producing potential achieved by one enterprise over others. Such conditions may have enormous value to individual business enterprises.

In our view, however, such intangibles do not constitute economic resources. They lack the basic characteristics of exchangeability and generally possess no power in exchange apart from the sale of the business as a whole. Further, their values are essentially unmeasurable since they relate almost solely to the uncertainties of future earnings. In a sense, the conversion of these intangible attributes into economic resources is what constitutes the earnings process.

Following our view, we would exclude from the balance sheet of a business enterprise deferred charges and other intangible assets not directly identified with economic resources or claims to future services, particularly when deferment is based solely on the expectation of matching such deferred amounts against future revenues. Economic resources may arise in the future from such expenditures, and this fact will be reflected in earnings. Only then have the expenditures been translated into assets (economic resources) that should be recognized in the balance sheet.

Measuring the "Value" of Economic Resources

In any formulation of financial statement objectives, it is not difficult to understand why emphasis should be placed upon value as the basis for measuring and communicating information with respect to economic resources and transactions related to such resources. Using value as a basis of measurement results in financial statements that more closely reflect economic realities and events as they exist and transpire.

Presentation of value-based information concerning economic resources in financial statements should be of primary relevance to (a) investors, (b) creditors and (c) others who use financial statements. This information indicates the economic strength of a business enterprise and, together with the historical record of its accomplishments, provides an important basis upon which to judge the capacity of the enterprise to produce and enhance its economic resources.

Economic decisions that arise from financial information concern the future. Financial statement users make assessments of the future that are based in part on information about current economic strength and past performance as displayed by the financial statements. This central role of financial statements will obviously best be served if such statements are based upon current data concerning values and changes in values of economic resources.

The value objective is sensible, not radical. We believe that this objective is intuitively held by a wide range of users of financial statements, including business managements, and by accountants who prepare statements. Much accounting literature has denied value as an objective, but the resolution of day-to-day accounting problems belies such literature. There is, for example, a continuous concern in accounting practice with one aspect of value. Is the asset at least worth its carrying value? Is its carrying value recoverable from future operations? Businessmen, accountants and knowledgeable users consider many balance sheets to be almost worthless in the sense of conveying meaningful information. Why is this true? It is because they do not regard the information as indicative of the value of the assets. Is not this attitude really a subtle acknowledgment of what our objectives are or should be?

Communicating the Substantive "Interests of Creditors"

The interests of creditors in existing economic resources may be those, for example, of employees for unpaid wages; of suppliers for goods, services or facilities delivered; of lenders for money provided; and of various governmental units for taxes of one kind or another.

In general, traditional accounting has relied too heavily on legal concepts to guide accounting practices for recognition of liabilities. While legal concepts should be considered, financial statements best serve the users when principal emphasis is placed on economic concepts. The recognition of a liability should be based on legal claims or substantive (even though not necessarily legally binding) claims for services, money, property, goods or facilities received by a reporting entity. For most types of obligations, the substantive approach results in the recognition of a liability at the time performance by the other party to the transaction occurs. Conversely, obligations or contracts that are contingent upon services to be rendered or goods or property to be furnished in the future by another party should not be recorded as liabilities because the obligations are contingent upon performance and do not need to be discharged until such performance has taken place.

Understanding the Nature of the "Equity of Owners in the Economic Resources"

While in our view the primary objective of financial statements is to convey information about the value of economic resources, that objective does not embrace reporting current-value information about the equity of owners. Accounting for the value of economic resources concerns the valuation of those individual assets of the business enterprises that have the characteristics of utility, scarcity and exchangeability. The owners' equity in these economic resources consists of their value less the entity's liabilities (i.e., the interests of creditors).

The difference between the owner's equity in the economic resources as shown in the financial statements and the market price that an investor pays for his equity interests in a business enterprise provides that investor with some essential data about the risks he takes with respect to the future—his wager on earning power.

Presenting the "Changes" in Economic Resources from Period to Period—The Earnings Concept

If earnings are to be considered a result of the measurement of economic resources, the periodic earnings will be determined by the change in the owners' equity as shown by comparative balance sheets (after provision for the maintenance of owners' capital to reflect the effects of inflation and after recognition of additional investments by owners and distributions to owners). In other words, the income or loss of an enterprise should be based upon the changes in value of that entity's net economic resources occurring during the period.

In the absence of evidence to the contrary, generally accepted accounting principles for financial reporting by business enterprises normally presume that the enterprise will continue to exist and function. Unless supported by the particular facts and circumstances, accounting should not communicate values of economic resources and interest of creditors under the assumption that an immediate termination of the enterprise will result.

Such a view, however, should not be interpreted to allow for an arbitrary "spreading" of costs or a "smoothing" of income. Changes from one date to another in the value of economic resources (exclusive of capital changes) represent an entity's earnings for the intervening period. Stability of earnings should not be communicated when there is, in fact, no such stability on the basis of the economic facts. It is not the function of accounting to ascertain and maintain an earnings trend—to "average out" unusual income or expense. Economic events or transactions should be accounted for in the period in which they occur in order to ensure that the economic resources as of a particular point in time are properly stated, and the interests of creditors and owners in these economic resources are properly reflected. The changes in the value of such resources will then be reflected in the period in which such changes actually occur.

For the statement of income to be presented in a form that will be of maximum assistance to the user in assessing the future, the following items should be set out separately (to the extent material in amount):

Operating earnings.

Financial expenses.

Charges for intangibles.

Provision for income taxes.

Unusual items not relevant to an assessment of future operating earnings.

Nonoperating holding gains or losses.

Provision for maintenance of capital.

In general, our recommendation to present separately the above items results from our desire to present financial statements in a form that is best suited to the investor's assessment of the future of the enterprise. For example, operating earnings should be segregated since such amounts are crucial in an assessment of management's performance and the related impact on future periods. Such earnings, in the normal case, should be expected to be continuing, as opposed to unusual items and nonoperating holding gains.

Application of our objectives can normally be expected to result in the expensing of intangible costs as incurred, and the separate disclosure of such costs provides additional information useful to the investor in his assessment of the value of intangible items and the value of the enterprise as a whole.

Finally, the provision for maintenance of capital results in the conversion of earnings from nominal terms to "real" terms. That is, the portion of the increases or decreases in reported amounts of net economic resources that results from changes in the general level of prices is segregated and eliminated in arriving at income for a period.

Overview of Impact of Our Financial Statement Objectives

If financial statement objectives do not follow the course described in the preceding pages, "assets" will be reported that are not represented by economic resources, or they will be reflected at amounts in excess of or less than their economic values. "Liabilities" will be recorded which differ from the interests of the creditors. The "changes" in the economic resources of an enterprise will not be communicated properly since reported earnings will differ from the actual amount of such changes. As a result, financial statement users will misinterpret the economic strengths of the business enterprise and will erroneously assess its capacity to produce and enhance its economic resources.

OUTMODED CONCEPTS AND PRACTICES

In explaining what we believe is the overall purpose of financial statements and identifying those financial statement objectives discussed above, we have deliberately rejected certain historic concepts and commonly accepted practices that, in our opinion, contribute significantly to present-day difficulties in accounting. Some of these concepts either never had much utility or have lost the utility they once possessed.

Cost As a Financial Statement Objective

First, there is the confusion of cost as an objective rather than a method. While cost was originally considered to be a useful measure of value, the transition was gradually made to the idea that cost should be used as such, and it became an objective in accounting. While we do not reject the usefulness cost serves in the measurement of the value of economic resources under some circumstances (e.g., at time of purchase), it must be viewed in this light rather than as an end in itself. In cases where cost is not relevant to the measurement of the value of economic resources, its use for this purpose must be rejected.

Conservatism

Financial statements should be prudently prepared. They should reflect soundly reasoned judgments on the basis of the best evidence available rather than mere hopes or speculations. This does not mean, however, that taking the most pessimistic view and understating economic resources—sometimes sanctioned as conservatism—are acceptable. Conservatism is a biased concept since it serves some financial statement users at the expense of others. For example, it seeks to protect the interests of the purchaser and the lender at the expense of the seller and the borrower. By communicating the value of economic resources and the changes in such values in the periods in which those changes actually occur, such bias is eliminated.

Objectivity at the Expense of Relevance

In the preparation of financial statements, there should be an appropriate balance between subjectivity, which contributes to relevance, and objectivity, which increases verifiability. Practice today is weighted far too heavily on the side of objectivity—almost to the extent of making objectivity an end rather than a means. For example, cost is justified as a method of measurement, even in instances when it differs significantly from value, on the basis that such a measurement method is "more objective."

The usefulness of financial statements will be increased as there is acceptance of the fact that the measurement, accumulation and summarization of the vast array of economic data about a business enterprise are highly subjective processes. Relatively little financial data should be interpreted as ironclad, indisputable fact, never subject to reevaluation. Accountants must acknowledge with greater emphasis that financial statements are always tentative and subject to change as significant additional facts emerge.

Earnings Stability

A final outmoded but commonly accepted practice that should be rejected, as noted earlier in this chapter, is the artificial leveling or smoothing of the trend in reported earnings. Stable growth in earnings is valued highly in the marketplace. If this stability is artificial, however, the result may be exaggerated market values for a company's stock. The truth is that changes in the value of economic resources come unevenly.

If the "ups" and "downs" in earnings were to be reported as they occur rather than being smoothed by various amortization techniques, the risks in business might be evaluated more realistically by the investor. The investor has a right to know about the fluctuations —the trend line is for him, not the accountant, to draw as a part of his analytical process in making investment decisions.

SIGNIFICANCE OF ABOVE OBJECTIVES TO CONCLUSIONS WITH RESPECT TO ACCOUNTING FOR PENSION PLANS AND THEIR COSTS

The present framework of generally accepted accounting principles is, in many respects, not consistent with our view of the objectives of financial statements. Accordingly, the accounting practices that flow from certain of our recommendations (both in general and in relation to pension plans and costs) would not be in conformity with generally accepted accounting principles as they exist today. Stated another way, we have not limited our proposals to the framework of existing practice. When we move into a discussion of accounting for pension plans and costs in Chapters 5, 6 and 7, we shall identify those proposals that could be implemented today and those that would require a more basic change in the presently existing framework of accounting.

chapter 4

Deficiencies in Present Practice—The Need for a Change

ALTHOUGH *APB Opinion No.* 8 represented a significant step forward when it was issued in 1966, it has outlived its usefulness. It was issued at a time when views with respect to financial statement objectives generally and with respect to pension costs specifically were less sophisticated than today. Many accountants were apprehensive about venturing into an unfamiliar territory long considered to be the domain of actuaries, and they were reluctant to promote their own views. Because of the complexities involved, the differences in views among accountants and the attempt to accommodate both the accounting and actuarial professions, *Opinion No.* 8 represented a compromise—a good compromise for its time but one that is no longer satisfactory.

Today, the pension environment has changed. Pension plans are far more significant than they were in 1966, both in terms of the number of employees covered and in the aggregate cost of such coverage. There is a dramatic need at the present time for revision of the accounting principles governing the accounting for the cost of pensions.

The changing pension environment has resulted in a dramatic increase in pension costs absorbed by employers. In response to the rapid increase in inflation experienced during the first half of this decade, plan amendments to liberalize benefits have been adopted with increasing frequency. Currently, U.S. companies are contributing an amount estimated to be equivalent to 15 percent of pretax profits to their pension funds—a sharp increase from prior years. The investment banking firm of Goldman, Sachs & Co. estimates that contributions will approximate 24 percent of pretax profits by 1978 and 30 percent by 1983.[1] The uneven investment performance of pension portfolios, combined with the trend toward liberalization of benefit provisions, has resulted in even more dramatic increases in the past-service liability and the obligation for vested benefits.[2]

ACCEPTANCE OF A VARIETY OF ACTUARIAL METHODS
AND AMORTIZATION PRACTICES

One of the most significant deficiencies in today's pension accounting under *APB Opinion No. 8* is the variety of widely differing patterns of cost recognition that can result when, under identical circumstances, an employer can apply any of a number of accepted actuarial cost methods.[3] These various methods differ in essential respects, such as whether future compensation levels are considered in determining current costs. They also differ in whether past-service costs are separately identified and, even more importantly, in the year-by-year relationship of resulting costs to employees' compensation.[4]

While most accountants and investment analysts recognize that various alternative actuarial cost methods are available under *APB Opinion No. 8* to account for similar pension transactions, few recognize the magnitude of the differences that these equally acceptable alternatives yield. The significance of such differences can be graphically illustrated on a general overview basis (for a typical plan assuming a 20 year amortization period for past-service costs) as shown:[5]

---

[1] Henry T. Blackstock, *Portfolio Comments: Higher Pension Costs Ahead* (New York: Goldman, Sachs & Co., December 1974), p. 5.

[2] Arlene Hershman, "The Big Pension Fund Drain" *Dun's Review*, vol. 106, no. 1 (July 1975), p. 34.

[3] For a description of the differing actuarial methods, see Appendix A of *APB Opinion No. 8.*

[4] For a more complete discussion of the various methods and examples of comparative cost recognition patterns, see Ernest L. Hicks, "Accounting for the Cost of Pension Plans," *Accounting Research Study No. 8* (New York: American Institute of Certified Public Accountants, 1965) Appendix C; Financial Accounting Standards Board, *Discussion Memorandum* (Stanford, Conn., 1975) Appendix C; and Dan M. McGill, *Fundamentals of Private Pensions*, 3d ed. (Homewood, Ill.: Richard D. Irwin, Inc., 1975), pp. 332–62.

[5] William A. Dreher, "Alternatives Available Under APB Opinion No. 8: An

Graphic Illustration of Differing Cost Patterns Obtained by Application of Differing Actuarial Cost Methods

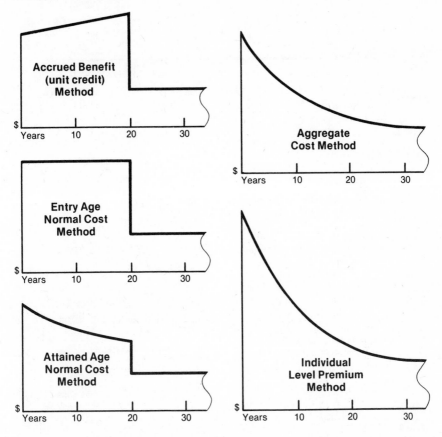

All of the actuarial cost methods illustrated are commonly used in practice at the present time.

The differing results set forth above are compounded by the *APB Opinion No.* 8 provision that allows for amortization of the unfunded past-service liability over any period ranging from about 10 to 40 years, while in certain instances no amortization is required.

Actuary's View," *The Journal of Accountancy*, vol. 124, no. 3 (September 1967) p. 41. This graphic illustration is admittedly not a precise representation of the results that could arise under each of the acceptable actuarial methods, but we believe that it is sufficient for our purposes in this monograph.

See C. L. Trowbridge, "Fundamentals of Pension Funding," *Transactions of the Society of Actuaries*, vol. IV (1952), p. 36, for a disclosure of the results over a representative period of time of applying the various actuarial methods to a typical simple-benefit-formula plan for 1,000 participants; those results are similar to results graphically illustrated by Dreher.

The following table shows the variety of practices that exist with respect to this alternative.[6]

Survey of Practices Employed by Companies Regarding Amortization of Pension Past-Service Costs

	Number of Firms			
	1968	1969	1970	1971
Amortization period (in years)				
10	2	2	1	1
11–20	6	6	6	7
21–30	31	33	35	33
31–40	19	19	19	19
No amortization	6	7	7	5
Other	2	2	2	1

While equally acceptable alternative methods of accounting exist for many other types of transactions, in most other cases the impact of the choice of methods can, at least to some extent, be assessed. When the last-in, first-out (Lifo) method of accounting for inventory costs is employed, the difference in inventory carrying amounts as compared with the first-in, first-out (Fifo) method is disclosed. When accelerated depreciation methods are used, that fact is disclosed and investors and other financial statement users will usually recognize the conservative impact which results as compared to the straight-line method. But this is not the case with respect to the alternative methods allowable in the accounting for pension plans. Few investors understand that the aggregate cost method results in drastically more rapid recognition of pension costs than the unit credit method—and even if they could recognize this point, the actuarial method used is not disclosed in financial statement notes.

During prior periods when pension costs typically represented no more than 5 percent or 10 percent of pretax income, perhaps the alternative practices did not significantly distort the financial statements of a business enterprise. But now pension costs typically exceed 15 percent or 20 percent of pretax income, and the flexibility of such accounting alternatives must be eliminated.

The accountant is not an actuary and has no expertise in how pension plans should be funded or in identifying and measuring turnover

[6] William C. Deaton and Jerry J. Weygandt, "Disclosures Related to Pension Plans," *The Journal of Accountancy*, vol. 139, no. 1 (January 1975), p. 46.

and other factors involved in actuarial determinations, but he has the responsibility for specifying the broad criteria for measuring assets, liabilities, revenues and expenses for financial-reporting purposes. The obligation to pay pension benefits does not change because of a change from one actuarial method to another.

FAILURE TO RECOGNIZE MOST OBLIGATIONS AS LIABILITIES

As noted in Chapter 2, APB *Opinion No. 8* does not generally require "unfunded prior service costs" to be treated as a liability. The rationale for this is strained and difficult to support on a logical basis. Some have relied upon legal concepts in contending that the liability for pension benefits need not be recognized by the employer until such liability is funded through contributions to the pension trust. They argue that the trust serves to insulate the employer from the legal liability.

For an ongoing plan, this argument has never been soundly based on the general concepts of accrual accounting, and the general thrust of ERISA serves further to strain the rationale for this legalistic view. No longer will it be possible for a continuing business enterprise to insulate itself fully from pension obligations by the use of a pension trust. Minimum funding and vesting requirements, as well as termination guarantee provisions contained in ERISA, serve to reduce this insulation. Because the employer is now required ultimately to fund those benefits defined in the plan, its obligation to provide the promised retirement benefits becomes more direct.

As explained in Chapter 3, we believe that a substantive liability arises and should be recognized in financial statements as performance in terms of delivering a product or rendering a service is completed. In the case of a pension plan, benefits are earned and a liability arises as service is rendered (i.e., as the employees' performance occurs). To the extent that employee service that enters into the determination of pension benefits estimated ultimately to be payable has already been rendered at the time a plan is adopted (or amended to increase benefits), an obligation exists and should be immediately recorded.

Does it make sense to wait until an expense is recognized under an arbitrary pattern to acknowledge a liability, particularly in view of the widely differing actuarial cost methods in use as discussed above?

ARTIFICIAL LEVELING OF EXPENSE

As discussed in Chapter 3, present accounting practice often places undue emphasis on the desirability of achieving a smooth or "normal" income level or trend even when such leveling is contrary to the economic facts and circumstances. Gains or losses that fall outside the assumed pattern are characterized as "distortive," and many accountants feel responsible for eliminating this "distortion" by adopting some leveling technique. This is usually justified as being more useful (but without saying to whom, or why) or as resulting in a better matching of revenues and costs.

This approach pervades APB Opinion No. 8. Most notably, it is the basis for the spreading of prior-service costs over a long future period—which, in turn, accounts for the failure to recognize the liability on a timely basis. It also serves as the rationale supporting the required spreading of actuarial gains and losses. As discussed in Chapter 3, increases and decreases in the value of economic resources should be accounted for in the periods in which they actually occur. Unfortunately, APB Opinion No. 8 does not provide this type of accounting recognition.

LATITUDE IN SELECTION OF ACTUARIAL ASSUMPTIONS

Finally, a weakness in present practice results from too great a degree of latitude in the application of actuarial assumptions. Although ERISA has narrowed the gap (to an extent not determinable pending the issuance of regulations), substantial leeway continues to exist. Many people, even generally knowledgeable ones, are amazed to learn that "it is a fairly sound generalization that in respect of a typical plan a change (upward or downward) of one percentage point in the interest assumption (e.g., an increase from 4 to 5 percent) alters the long-run cost estimate by about 25 percent."[7] Variations in other assumptions—for example, those relating to employee turnover and salary rate increases—also can create major pension cost changes. Estimates as to the future inflation rate implicitly contained in the salary rate and interest assumptions are particularly sensitive to change.[8]

---

[7] FASB, Discussion Memorandum, p. C-8.

[8] Howard E. Winklevoss, Pension Mathematics: With Numerical Illustrations (Homewood, Ill.: Richard D. Irwin, Jan. 1977) chapter 15.

Selection of assumptions, of course, requires judgment, and judgments will differ. So do circumstances. There should not be a straitjacket imposed on actuarial assumptions, but we do need criteria for guiding and narrowing the range of selections. As pension costs become more significant to business enterprises, such criteria become increasingly important. The actuarial profession may need to do further work in this area following issuance of ERISA regulations.

chapter 5

An Overview of Accounting
for Pension Plans

ONE COULD MOVE directly at this point into a discussion of how companies that sponsor pension plans for their employees should account for the cost of such plans. We have chosen, instead, to consider first the appropriate accounting for the plans themselves as separate reporting entities. In this chapter, we shall discuss generally our views with respect to accounting for pension plans; in the next chapter, we shall consider in some depth the manner in which we believe that pension obligation accruals should be correlated with performance by employees.

ERISA has recognized pension plans as accounting and reporting entities. Partly as a result of the reporting requirements imposed by ERISA, the FASB established its project on pension plan accounting and reporting. As previously noted, at the time of this writing the FASB has issued a *Discussion Memorandum*[1] and held a public hearing but has not issued an exposure draft of a financial accounting standard with respect to the subject.

While making it clear that the accounting for pension costs by sponsoring companies is a separate matter,[2] the *Discussion Memo-*

---

[1] FASB, *Discussion Memorandum* (Stamford, Conn., 1975). As with all FASB discussion memorandums, this one dealing with accounting for pension plans is neutral in not expressing or intending to imply conclusions; it identifies issues for consideration and presents arguments from various viewpoints on each.

[2] The FASB has also created a project and established a task force on accounting and reporting for pension costs but, at the time of this writing, has not issued a discussion memorandum on the subject.

randum suggested that respondents bear in mind the possibility that symmetry between the accounting and reporting followed by a pension plan and that followed by a sponsoring employer might be appropriate.[3] We consider such symmetry to be appropriate, and it is for this reason we have concluded that it is logical to discuss pension plan accounting here. Although present practice is diverse in many respects, we consider the approach that we recommend to be in accordance with generally accepted accounting principles as they presently exist.

RELATIONSHIP OF FINANCIAL STATEMENT OBJECTIVES TO PENSION PLANS

We have set forth in Chapter 3 our views regarding financial statement objectives because we strongly believe that identification of such objectives should precede any formulation of more specific accounting standards governing pension transactions. Others, both within and outside of the accounting profession, have adopted similar approaches.[4]

As we discussed in Chapter 3, we believe that the overall objective of financial statements is to communicate information concerning the nature and value of the economic resources of an entity as of a specified date, the interests of various parties in such resources as of that date and the changes in the nature and value of those resources from period to period. Users of financial statements of pension plans are adequately served by this overall objective. The perspective and needs of the financial statement users can be more sharply defined in this case, however, since such users are dealing with only one broad type of economic transaction—the transfer of benefits from an employer to its employees.

The Specific Needs of Pension Plan Financial Statement Users

The perspective of the financial statement users is in part affected by the distinctions between a *defined benefit* plan (that is, a plan

---

[3] FASB, *Discussion Memorandum*, pp. 3–4.

[4] For example, Preston C. Bassett, in our view, properly stressed the need to consider ". . . really elementary issues of accounting and reporting . . . who uses what information . . ." in the formulation of conclusions as to the proper accounting and reporting for employee benefit plans. "Who What and When of Accounting and Reporting for Pension Plans," *Financial Executive*, vol. XLIV, no. 1 (January 1976),

that defines the amount of benefits to be received by employees, without regard to the amount of employer contributions required) and a *defined contribution* plan (that is, a plan that provides a formula for determining the amount of the employer's contributions, which contributions plus fund earnings will result in the benefits the employees will receive).

Under a defined benefit plan, the rights of the participants are normally not directly affected by changes in the economic resources of the plan; the sponsoring employer, in effect, bears the risks of ownership of the plan's assets.[5] The employer is concerned with the earnings performance and the risk attributes associated with these assets, and the related impact on future funding requirements. The employee's basic concern is, "How secure are my benefits as defined?" He wants to know whether the assets of the plan provide sufficient security with respect to these benefits, or whether he must secondarily look through the plan to the financial soundness of the sponsoring company in evaluating this security.

On the other hand, in a defined contribution plan, the perspectives of the sponsoring employer and participating employees are different from those in a defined benefit plan. The employer is not as directly affected by the earning performance and risk attributes of the plan's assets, since the ownership risks attributable to these assets are, in effect, assumed by the participant. It is the participant who principally needs this information about plan assets in order to evaluate not only the security of his benefits but also the estimated amount of benefits and, in certain cases, the adequacy of the funding of the intended benefits.

While the needs of any particular group of financial statement users may be affected significantly by the type of employee benefit plan being accounted for, the needs of all financial statement users considered in the aggregate do not change. There is merely a shift in emphasis; that is, the information that may be important primarily to one group of financial statement users (for example, the

---

p. 12. (It is acknowledged, however, that Mr. Bassett's conclusions with respect to the accounting and reporting for pension plans differ substantially from those we are setting forth in this chapter.)

[5] Variable annuities are an exception under which the employee bears the investment risk under a defined benefit plan while the employer bears the risk with respect to mortality, turnover, salary increases, etc.

employers) under one type of plan becomes important primarily to another group of users (for example, the employees) under another type of plan. Under any plan, some financial statement users will desire information with which to assess (a) security of benefits, (b) adequacy of funding and (c) investment performance. Financial statement objectives should be responsive to these needs.

As is the case with any financial statements, users may have differing emphases in their interests, and some will always want more detail than others. This goes, however, to method and detail of presentation, and these differing requirements as to the amount of detail presented should not affect the identification or measurement of assets and liabilities—or changes in assets or liabilities from period to period.

Information Required to Satisfy the Plan Financial Statement Users' Needs

In order to be responsive to these needs, the financial statements of a pension plan must contain information about the nature and value of the plan's economic resources and the changes in such resources from period to period. In addition, information about plan obligations is also of utmost importance.

The accrual basis of accounting is consistent with generally accepted accounting principles, as well as with the objectives that we have identified, and this basis should be employed in the accounting and reporting for pension plans. The accrual basis is employed presently in accounting for similar entities; for example, the AICPA Industry Audit Guides, *Audits of Investment Companies*[6] and *Audits of Voluntary Health and Welfare Organizations*,[7] both provide for accrual accounting. The cash basis of accounting may yield distorted or incomplete results that are not consistent with financial statement objectives as they relate to pension plans, as set forth earlier in this chapter. Subject to materiality considerations, the cash basis, or any "modified cash" or "modified accrual" basis, is not acceptable.

Generally accepted accounting principles for financial reporting by

---

[6] American Institute of Certified Public Accountants, "Audits of Investment Companies," *Industry Audit Guide* (New York, 1973).

[7] American Institute of Certified Public Accountants, "Audits of Voluntary Health and Welfare Organizations," *Industry Audit Guide* (New York, 1974).

other entities normally presume that the entity will continue to exist and function, unless contrary evidence arises. This concept is equally relevant for the financial statements of a pension plan. The assessment of the security of plan benefits should not be based upon an assumption of plan termination if such termination is not likely to occur. Similarly, the need for information to enable assessment of the adequacy of funding and/or investment performance would not effectively be met if the financial statements assumed termination and that event were not likely to occur.

Although the financial statements should be responsive to the needs of the users, it must be recognized that such needs can only be satisfied within the constraints and limitations underlying the nature of the information that is subject to accounting and reporting in financial statements. For example, whereas pension plan financial statements should provide information with which a user can assess the future security of plan benefits, the statements should not attempt to present a projection or prediction of future assets or unearned obligations. While the valuation of presently existing assets and obligations is often dependent, at least in part, on an assessment of future events and transactions, this integral part of the accounting valuation process for currently existing assets and obligations should be differentiated from projections or predictions of the amounts of assets or obligations that may arise in the future but that do not currently exist. Projections or predictions of such assets or obligations should be made by the user utilizing the information from the financial statements with respect to economic events and transactions that have, in fact, occurred and can be accounted for.

CURRENT VALUE METHOD OF ASSET MEASUREMENT

The various classes of assets of a pension plan should be accounted for using current value as a measurement basis. As indicated previously, current value accounting is consistent with our views concerning overall objectives of financial statements. Specifically with respect to pension plans, information about the value of the plan's economic resources is relevant to (a) an evaluation of the extent to which employees' rights to pension benefits are secure, (b) an evaluation of earnings performance of the plan's assets and (c) an evaluation by the employer of the adequacy of funding. Historical asset cost has no particular relationship to a plan's ability to meet its obligations for present and future benefits. Consequently, use of the current-value basis better accomplishes the objectives described previously relating to both financial position and periodic changes in such financial position. For defined contribution plans which calculate benefit payments based upon current fund values, the relevance of current-value accounting (and the lack of relevance of historical-cost accounting) becomes particularly obvious.

We believe that the practices used by investment companies in valuing investment securities have been successful, and provide a sound basis for use in accounting for pension plan assets. These procedures, which provide for (a) valuation of securities for which market quotations are readily available at the quoted market price and (b) valuation of other securities and assets at fair value as determined in good faith by the board of directors, are described in SEC *Accounting Series Release No. 118*[8] and in the AICPA Industry Audit Guide, *Audits of Investment Companies.*[9]

Some contend that valuation of plan assets at current value is not compatible with actuarial valuations of pension obligations. Such actuarial methods typically involve a spreading of actuarial and investment gains and losses and employ interest assumptions different from those implicit in valuing fixed income securities at market. We believe that such apparent inconsistencies are reconciled when the purposes of the data involved in each method are considered. The current-value approach should be used to measure a plan's financial position *at a single point in time* and for past periods—to measure the plan's resources at that point in time, and the extent to which these resources compare with the plan's obligation for estimated benefits. On the other hand, actuarial techniques are used to project total pension benefits *over a period of time,* and the funding required during that period to meet the estimated obligations. The concepts of spreading gains and losses and making long-term interest and other actuarial assumptions (which may differ from circumstances as of a particular date) are valid when dealing with best estimates of what will occur over a future period of time. However, such con-

---

[8] Securities and Exchange Commission, *Accounting Series Release No. 118,* "Investment Company Act of 1940—Accounting for Investment Securities by Registered Investment Companies" (Washington, D.C., December 23, 1970).

[9] AICPA, "Audits of Investment Companies," *Industry Audit Guide,* 1973.

cepts are not relevant to a measure of actual resources as of a particular date or actual operating results for a particular reporting period.

This does not mean, however, that the valuation of plan assets and the measurement of pension obligations are separate and unrelated matters. The effective yields (realized and unrealized) that are implicit in asset valuations are an important factor to be considered in establishing the discount rate to be used in measuring the pension obligation. This is discussed later under the caption, "Obligation Should Be Recorded on Present Value Basis."

NEED TO RECOGNIZE OBLIGATION FOR PENSION BENEFITS

Clearly, disclosure of some measure of the obligation for pension benefits is in accordance with the objectives we believe are relevant in accounting and reporting for employee benefit plans. The obligation is vital in the user's evaluation of (a) the extent to which the participants' rights to benefits are secure and (b) the extent of future funding which may be required. Disclosure is best presented by reporting *the value of accrued benefits earned to date as an obligation in the plan's balance sheet*. In addition, disclosure of the portion of the above obligation that is represented by vested benefits should also be made, either on the face of the balance sheet or supplementally in a note.

To determine whether the obligation should be reflected as a liability or as plan equity, we believe that the underlying terms of the plan should be examined to determine if it is a defined benefit or a defined contribution plan. As we have previously indicated, under a defined contribution plan the risks of ownership of the resources of the plan usually flow to the employee participants. Consequently, the participants' benefits are similar to rights of shareholders, and the plan's obligation to meet these rights can be viewed as the plan's equity. Conversely, under a defined benefit plan the benefits are fixed and, therefore, represent a liability to outside parties. The sponsoring employer effectively assumes the equity risks of asset ownership. In either case, recognition of the obligation for benefits earned in the financial statements is most important as this treatment will disclose the amount by which the plan assets exceed or are less than such obligation (or that the assets are equal to the obligation if that is the case)—an important piece of financial information to financial statement users.

Some have contended that recording estimates of future benefits based upon actuarial calculations is subject to too much future revision to be meaningful and would be interpreted by financial statement users as being more precise than is warranted. We see no difference between these types of estimates and others that are required in existing accounting practice (e.g., estimates of insurance company reserves and warranty reserves). Many accounting principles in other areas are predicated upon accounting estimates and, consistent with these principles, a "best efforts" approach should be adopted.

BASIS FOR RECORDING OBLIGATION FOR PENSION BENEFITS

Obligation Should Not Assume Plan Termination

Measurement of the obligation should not assume termination of the plan. Such an assumption would be contrary to the underlying premise upon which accounting for employee benefit plans should be based. Plan terminations are not typical, and to assume otherwise would result in providing information that is inconsistent with the needs of the financial statement users. If, of course, termination becomes imminent, the measurement basis should be changed accordingly, just as would be the case in other accounting and financial reporting situations in the event of termination.

Obligation Should Be Based on Service Rendered to Date by Present Participants

The obligation for plan benefits should be measured in a manner consistent with the determination of any other liability. As discussed previously, recognition of a liability should be based upon substantive as well as legal claims. As performance is completed, a liability is incurred. Conversely, obligations or contracts that are contingent upon services to be rendered or goods or property to be furnished in the future by another party should not be recorded as liabilities because such obligations are contingent upon performance and do not need to be discharged until such performance has taken place.

Applying these concepts to the accounting and reporting for pension plans, we believe that an obligation for plan benefits should be recorded in pension plan financial statements as such benefits are *earned* by the employees—that is, as the employees' performance, as measured by service rendered to date, has been completed. This applies regardless of how the pension obligation is ultimately determined (e.g., average compensation, formula related to final compensation, or even some method unrelated to direct compensation).

In concluding that a substantive liability results from benefits earned by employees' performance, we view the liability of the plan as relating to the present group of employees as a whole. For a single employee, there can be a serious question whether a substantive liability, much less a legally binding one, arises as he or she performs services; there are too many uncertainties (death, termination of employment, future earnings levels, etc.) for a reasonable estimate to be made and recorded. For the group as a whole, however, experience and actuarial techniques make possible a reasonable estimation that is compatible with—in fact, required by—accrual accounting.

A liability does not exist for aggregate total future benefits estimated ultimately to be payable to present employees to the extent that such benefits have not yet been earned. Unearned estimated future benefits are simply a commitment of the plan—a commitment that is executory in nature and dependent on future performance by the employees. The translation of this commitment into a fixed obligation that should be recorded does not occur until performance occurs—that is, until the employees' service results in the benefits being earned.

Similarly, any obligation to future plan participants does not arise until the future period in which such employees enter the plan and begin to perform services. Since no services have been performed and, hence, no substantive claim exists until that time, no liability should be recorded in anticipation of the future. As the new employees enter the plan, they will begin earning their pension benefits, and the related obligation will begin to be recorded as a function of the compensation costs incurred.

To the extent that employee service that enters into the determination of pension benefits estimated ultimately to be payable has already been rendered at the time a plan is adopted (or amended to increase benefits), an obligation with respect to that service exists and should be immediately recorded. Although one may argue as far as the *employer* is concerned that the obligation arising from past or prior service relates to expected future service and, hence, that the contra cost relates to future periods (a matter that will be considered in Chapter 7), there is no basis for the *plan* not to recognize the obligation when it is incurred.

Obligation for Service Rendered to Date Should Be Measured on Basis of Compensation

In determining how to measure benefits earned by employees on the basis of service rendered to date, we considered two methods of identifying "service rendered to date"—one, on the basis of time, and the other, on the basis of direct compensation. The time approach would relate the pension accrual to the portion of estimated total years of service that an employee has worked to date, whereas the direct-compensation approach would base the accrual on the proportion of estimated career compensation that has been earned to date.

The time basis has some appeal and logical support, especially where plan benefits are not based on compensation. It is sometimes argued that the use of a compensation base is irrelevant and arbitrary with that type of plan. Furthermore, the time basis results in a level accrual (before giving effect to discounting), which has a practical appeal to some—especially in contrast to the compensation basis, which produces an increasing accrual and, in the view of some, is not sufficiently conservative.

On the other hand, it can be argued that, since pension costs are a part of the total compensation package, it is logical to measure the obligation for pension benefits earned to date on the basis of direct compensation. Direct compensation measures the value of services rendered (i.e., performance), and the pension cost portion of total compensation should be accrued on the basis of performance.

We have weighed the arguments with respect to these two approaches to measuring service rendered to date for the purpose of accruing pension obligations and have concluded that the most appropriate method of measuring that portion of benefits that has been earned to date is to correlate the recording of the obligation with employee compensation costs. Economically, employees' compensation is the best indication of when the earning process takes place and, consequently, the pension obligation should be recorded proportionately as the direct compensation cost is incurred. The fact that the mechanics of computing benefits under the plan may not be the same is not relevant to the determination of annual accruals, and the fact that the compensation basis results in an increasing pattern of accruals is similarly of no relevance in arriving at the appropriate result.

The general considerations involved in correlating the accrual of pension obligations with employee compensation costs are discussed in the remainder of this chapter. Chapter 6 consists of a detailed discussion, with illustrations, of the manner in which the correlation should be effected.

Obligation Recorded Periodically Should Give Consideration to Benefits Estimated Ultimately to Be Payable

Although the obligation to be recorded should not reflect an anticipation of any service not yet performed by employees, estimated future compensation levels (including increases resulting from inflation) should be considered in measuring the obligation. This, we believe, is true in all cases but is most readily apparent where the amount of the benefit ultimately payable is dependent on some future consideration—for example, on average earnings during the last five years prior to retirement. Such a consideration of expected future salary increases does not represent an anticipation of an obligation not yet incurred, but does represent another factor to be considered in an estimate of the amount of the benefits ultimately expected to be payable, just as estimated inflation implicit in the discount rate and estimated mortality, disability and employee turnover must be considered.[10]

Once an estimate of the total benefits ultimately expected to be payable has been made, the liability for such benefits should be recognized only as "earned" by employees, measured by a correlation with presently existing employee compensation costs as discussed

---

[10] This distinction between anticipation of a future event, on the one hand, and giving consideration to it, on the other, is, perhaps, more clearly illustrated with respect to depreciation. One does not anticipate (in the accounting sense of recording as an asset) the estimated proceeds to be received from salvage of a property item at the end of its useful life, but one does give consideration to estimated salvage, as well as estimated useful life, in establishing the depreciation rate to be applied during its life.

in Chapter 6, "Correlation of Pension Obligation with Employee Compensation."

Obligation Should Be Recorded on Present-Value Basis

Recording the obligation on a present-value basis is necessary and is consistent with existing accounting principles as set forth in *APB Opinion No. 21*[11] and *APB Opinion No. 12*[12]. From an economic standpoint, a present-value basis results in an appropriate measure of the amount of the obligation to be recorded since the benefits arising from the pension obligation will not be paid until the participants retire and, in the meanwhile, plan assets arising from contributions to the plan will likely be earning a return. We recognize that unsettled questions exist in present accounting practice regarding the extent to which present-value concepts should be applied in the valuation of assets and liabilities, but the present-value approach is clearly applicable to the determination of pension obligations.

Several factors should be considered in establishing the discount rate. For purposes of determining pension obligations, one of the most significant of these factors is the total investment return (including realized and unrealized appreciation) upon the current carrying amount of the plan's investment portfolio. As discussed above under "Current Value Method of Asset Measurement," we do not consider the valuation of plan assets and the measurement of pension obligations to be unrelated matters.[13] The concern some

---

[11] American Institute of Certified Public Accountants, "Interest on Receivables and Payables," *APB Opinion No. 21* (New York, 1971).

[12] American Institute of Certified Public Accountants, "Omnibus Opinion—1967," *APB Opinion No. 12* (New York, 1967).

[13] For a contrary view, see John F. Dewhirst, "A Conceptual Approach to Pension Accounting," *The Accounting Review*, vol. XLVI, no. 2 (April 1971). Professor Dewhirst presents cogent arguments for using the sponsor's cost of capital, concluding that "[o]ver time, the difference between interest expense on the pension liability calculated at the cost of capital rate, and the earnings rate on the pension fund, represents a measure of the cost of investing company funds in traditionally low-earning assets."

Although recognizing the persuasiveness of some of the supporting arguments, we have adopted a different viewpoint. First, while endorsing the general principle of symmetry between accounting for pension plans and accounting for pension costs, we are unwilling to go as far as Professor Dewhirst in considering plan assets and obligations to be directly those of the company. Second, in the absence of reason to believe that any significant distortion might result from coordinating the discount rate with investment return, we have opted for such coordination on the basis of understandability and simplicity.

accountants and actuaries have expressed about valuing plan assets at current market is that this distorts the perceived relationship between the two. It is argued that, if plan assets earn a total return that will fund pension obligations when they become due, there is no reason to create periodic gains and losses for accounting purposes by revaluations of assets. This argument, however, ignores the possibility of revising the discount rate used in measuring the pension obligation to reflect the changes in total return reflected in changed asset values.

In the final analysis, we believe that the discount rate used in measuring pension obligations should be coordinated with the return on fund assets. This should be accomplished by changing the assumed discount rate from time to time as required to reflect the changing return on assets at current value rather than by "freezing" a matching at some return and discount rate that may lose any current significance with the passage of time. This does not, however, imply a need for continuous "fine tuning" of the discount rate to reflect each and every change in returns as general interest rates and specific factors affecting fund assets fluctuate. In addition, factors other than asset return should be considered in determining the discount rate to be used.

One of these other factors to consider in establishing the discount rate is the extent of risk inherent in the investment portfolio. The discount rate should not be adjusted, for example, merely because an investment decision is made to substitute lower-rated fixed-income securities for other securities that are AAA rated, since the higher yield associated with the lower rated securities reflects the increased risk associated with such securities and does not necessarily mean that a higher ultimate return on the aggregate investment portfolio will result.

Finally, the consistency of the assumption of future inflation implicitly contained in the discount rate with that included in the actuarial salary rate assumption should be considered.

Obligation Should Give Current Recognition to Changes in Actuarial Assumptions

Consistent with our view of the nature of a liability, we believe that pension obligations should reflect the accrued benefits earned to date determined on the basis of current actuarial assumptions. The effect of changes in actuarial assumptions should be recognized in the financial statements as they arise—i.e., without any deferral and amortization of resulting gains or losses.

Obligation Should Not Be Less Than the Vested Benefits

The recorded obligation, measured by following the principles set forth above and employing the specific method of correlation with compensation outlined in Chapter 6, will usually exceed the obligation that has been incurred to date for vested benefits. However, if instances occur where this is not the result, the recorded obligation should not be less than the obligation for vested benefits determined under the terms of the plan. By definition, when vesting occurs an obligation arises that is not contingent upon future performance by the employee—performance has already taken place.

TREATMENT OF DIFFERENCE BETWEEN PLAN'S ASSETS AND RECORDED OBLIGATION

In a defined benefit plan, the value of the funded assets of the plan will normally differ from the liability amount recorded in recognition of the obligation for benefits earned to date by participating employees. Since the risk of ownership of the plan's assets runs to the employer and since the obligation for plan benefits represents a fixed commitment to an outsider (employee) group unaffected by any ownership risks, it follows that the resulting difference between the two amounts represents an equity interest (or deficit obligation) of the employer. Because the plan is viewed as a separate reporting unit, rather than merely as a nonentity conduit of the employer, this balancing figure should be represented as a fund balance (or deficit) in the equity section of the balance sheet rather than as a receivable from or payable to the employer company. That treatment, however, does not change the substantive interest in (or obligation of) the employer for such amount.

Of course, the facts of a defined contribution plan differ. In such plans the obligation to employees, by definition, is normally equal to the plan's assets. That amount represents equity of the *employees* because it is the employees, and not the employers, who assume the risk of ownership of the plan assets.

ACTUARIAL ASSUMPTIONS

In Chapter 4, we discussed a weakness in present practice that results from too great a degree of latitude in the application of actuarial assumptions in the measurement of the estimated pension obligation. Selection of appropriate assumptions requires a great deal of judgment, and no accounting rules should be established that restrict the ability to exercise such judgment.

Selection of reasonable actuarial assumptions is of utmost importance. In our view, the reasonableness of such assumptions will best be assured if a proper communication is established among the parties who participate in this decision-making process. Management's participation, together with that of the actuary, will be beneficial in this regard in that the judgment of both of these parties can be exercised in a coordinated effort in reaching a best estimate of the most reasonable assumptions. It is important that both parties understand the accounting and reporting objectives relevant to the measure of the pension obligation and how these objectives may differ from the objectives of pension funding.

ERISA requires that the actuary be satisfied that, in the aggregate, the actuarial assumptions employed in computing the estimated pension obligation are reasonably related to the past experience of the plan, and represent a reasonable expectation of anticipated future experience. The independent auditor should obtain an understanding of the assumptions used in the actuarial computations. In obtaining this understanding, the auditor will normally be required to discuss with management and the actuaries the bases for determining the reasonableness of such assumptions.

chapter 6

Correlation of Pension Obligation with Employee Compensation

As DISCUSSED in Chapter 5, the accrual of the obligation for pension benefits should be correlated with employee performance as measured by compensation. We shall consider two methods by which such a correlation can be accomplished—methods that are based on different fundamental concepts and that produce significantly different accrual patterns. One of these methods consists of correlating the *cost* of benefits with compensation; the other consists of correlating the pension *benefits* with compensation.

Although both of these methods appear to be substantially the same as actuarial methods used in practice and/or described in literature dealing with pension funding techniques, we have chosen in the discussion that follows to describe them by using our own nomenclature rather than by using actuarial funding terminology. We are following this course for two reasons—first, because we approached our study from an accounting viewpoint without regard to what actuarial method, if any, might be used to derive or approximate the measurement pattern we propose; and, second, because we are not actuaries and wish to avoid labeling our conclusions with actuarial terms that might have additional implications of which we are unaware. If our views find support, we shall leave it to members of the actuarial profession to identify or devise actuarial methods of application.

CORRELATION OF THE COST OF BENEFITS
WITH COMPENSATION

Under the method in which the cost of the pension obligation is correlated with compensation, a determination is first made of the percentage relationship of (a) the present values at retirement date of the estimated pension benefits to (b) the accumulated value of total estimated compensation to retirement. The resulting percentage is then applied to each year's compensation to determine the accrual based on compensation. At the end of each year, the accrued obligation consists of the accruals to date based on compensation plus interest on the obligation accrued to date, less benefit payments to date.

This method is illustrated for a single participant in Table 1. For simplicity in appraising the result of the cost-correlation method, it is assumed that compensation remains constant throughout the period.

Assumptions for Table 1

Hired—January 1, 1976
Retirement date—December 31, 1995
Discount rate, including an allowance both for an interest factor
    and for population decrements—12%
Present value at retirement date of estimated pension benefits:

Base—average earnings for final three years prior
    to retirement $10,000
Annual pension—50% of base 5,000
Present value at retirement date, at 6%, assuming
    benefits will be paid at the end of each year for
    12 years subsequent to the retirement date
    ($5,000 × 8.38384394) 41,919

It is unrealistic, of course, to assume a constant level of compensation for an employee throughout any prolonged period of employment. The same approach followed in Table 1 is applicable where an increasing level of compensation throughout an employee's period of service is assumed. This is illustrated in Table 2.

Assumptions for Table 2

Hired—January 1, 1976
Retirement date—December 31, 1995

TABLE 1

Illustration of Pension Accrual for a Single Participant Derived by Correlating the Cost of Benefits with Compensation (assuming level compensation)

(1)	(2)	(3)	(4)	(5)	(6) Accrued Obligation	(7)	(8)
Year	Annual Compensation	Amount That $1 Will Accumulate at Retirement	Product of (2) × (3)	Accrual Based on Compensation (2) × 5.8178%*	Beginning of Year	Discount Rate Applied to Beginning Balance	End of Year (5) + (6) + (7)
1976	$10,000	$8.61276169	$ 86,128	$581	$ —	$ —	$ 581
1977	10,000	7.68996579	76,900	581	581	69	1,231
1978	10,000	6.86604088	68,660	581	1,231	148	1,960
1979	10,000	6.13039365	61,304	581	1,960	236	2,777
1980	10,000	5.47356575	54,736	581	2,777	334	3,692
1981	10,000	4.88711228	48,871	581	3,692	444	4,717
1982	10,000	4.36349311	43,635	581	4,717	567	5,865
1983	10,000	3.89597599	38,960	581	5,865	705	7,151
1984	10,000	3.47854999	34,785	581	7,151	859	8,591
1985	10,000	3.10584820	31,058	581	8,591	1,032	10,204
1986	10,000	2.77307875	27,731	581	10,204	1,226	12,011
1987	10,000	2.47596317	24,760	581	12,011	1,443	14,035
1988	10,000	2.21068140	22,107	581	14,035	1,686	16,302
1989	10,000	1.97382268	19,738	581	16,302	1,958	18,841
1990	10,000	1.76234168	17,623	581	18,841	2,263	21,685
1991	10,000	1.57351936	15,735	581	21,685	2,604	24,870
1992	10,000	1.40492800	14,049	581	24,870	2,986	28,437
1993	10,000	1.25440000	12,544	581	28,437	3,414	32,432
1994	10,000	1.12000000	11,200	581	32,432	3,894	36,907
1995	10,000	1.00000000	10,000	581	36,907	4,431	41,919
			$720,524				

* Percentage of (a) the present value of estimated pension benefits at December 31, 1995, to (b) the accumulated value of compensation to December 31, 1995—
$41,919 ÷ $720,524 = 5.8178%.

TABLE 2

Illustration of Pension Accrual for a Single Participant Derived by Correlating the Cost of Benefits with Compensation (assuming increasing compensation)

(1)	(2)	(3)	(4)	(5)	(6) Accrued Obligation	(7)	(8)
Year	Annual Compensation	Amount That $1 Will Accumulate at Retirement	Product of (2) × (3)	Accrual Based on Compensation (2) × 13.4672%*	Beginning of Year	Discount Rate Applied to Beginning Balance	End of Year (5) + (6) + (7)
1976	$10,000	$8.61276169	$ 86,128	$1,347	$ —	$ —	$ 1,347
1977	10,800	7.68996579	83,052	1,454	1,347	162	2,963
1978	11,664	6.86604088	80,086	1,571	2,963	356	4,890
1979	12,597	6.13039365	77,225	1,696	4,890	587	7,173
1980	13,605	5.47356575	74,468	1,832	7,173	861	9,866
1981	14,693	4.88711228	71,806	1,979	9,866	1,184	13,029
1982	15,869	4.36349311	69,244	2,137	13,029	1,562	16,728
1983	17,138	3.89597599	66,769	2,308	16,728	2,007	21,043
1984	18,509	3.47854999	64,384	2,493	21,043	2,525	26,061
1985	19,990	3.10554820	62,086	2,692	26,061	3,127	31,880
1986	21,589	2.77307875	59,868	2,907	31,880	3,826	38,613
1987	23,316	2.47596317	57,730	3,140	38,613	4,634	46,387
1988	25,182	2.21068140	55,669	3,391	46,387	5,566	55,344
1989	27,196	1.97382268	53,680	3,663	55,344	6,641	65,648
1990	29,372	1.76234168	51,764	3,956	65,648	7,878	77,482
1991	31,722	1.57351936	49,915	4,272	77,482	9,298	91,052
1992	34,259	1.40492800	48,131	4,614	91,052	10,927	106,593
1993	37,000	1.25440000	46,413	4,983	106,593	12,791	124,367
1994	39,960	1.12000000	44,755	5,381	124,367	14,924	144,672
1995	43,157	1.00000000	43,157	5,812	144,672	17,361	167,845
			$1,246,330				

* Percentage of (a) the present value of estimated pension benefits at December 31, 1995, to (b) the accumulated value of estimated compensation to December 31, 1995—
$167,845 ÷ $1,246,330 = 13.4672%.

Compensation increase—8% annually compounded (includes increases assumed to result from inflation)

Discount rate, including an allowance both for an interest factor and for population decrements—12%

Present value at retirement date of estimated pension benefits:

Base—average earnings for final three years prior
  to retirement .... $ 40,039
Annual pension—50% of base   20,020
Present value at retirement date, at 6%, assuming
  benefits will be paid at the end of each year for
  12 years subsequent to the retirement date
  ($20,020 × 8.38384394)   167,845

As with Table 1, this method of determining an annual accrual derived by correlating the *cost* of pension benefits with compensation results in an annual accrual (Column 5) that remains a constant percentage of the employee's compensation (Column 2) throughout the period of employment—hence the term "cost-correlation."

CORRELATION OF THE PENSION BENEFITS WITH COMPENSATION

Another method of correlating the accrual of the obligation for pension benefits with employee performance as measured by compensation is to relate the pension benefits (rather than the cost of such benefits) to compensation. Under this approach, the percentage of (a) the present value at retirement date of the estimated pension benefits to (b) the total estimated compensation to retirement is first determined. This percentage is then applied to each year's compensation in order to allocate the pension *benefits* on the basis of compensation. The benefit at retirement date that is allocated to each year is then discounted to present value for that year. The amount so determined represents the accrual based on compensation; and, at the end of each year, the accrued obligation consists of the accruals to date based on compensation plus interest on the obligation accrued to date, less benefit payments to date.

Again, as with the cost-correlation method, this benefit-correlation method is first illustrated in Table 3 for a single participant whose compensation remains constant throughout the period of employment. The assumptions are the same as were employed in Table 1.

TABLE 3

Illustration of Pension Accrual for a Single Participant Derived by Correlating the Pension Benefits with Compensation (assuming level compensation)

(1)	(2)	(3)	(4)	(5)	(6)	(7)	(8)
		Correlation of Pension Benefit with Compensation	Present Value of $1 Payable at Retirement	Accrual Based on Present Value of Pension Benefits	Accrued Obligation		End of Year
Year	Annual Compensation	(2) × 20.95959%*		(3) × (4)	Beginning of Year	Discount Rate Applied to Beginning Balance	(5) + (6) + (7)
1976	$ 10,000	$2,096	$ .116106	$ 243	$ —	$ —	$ 243
1977	10,000	2,096	.130039	273	243	29	545
1978	10,000	2,096	.145644	305	545	65	915
1979	10,000	2,096	.163121	342	915	110	1,367
1980	10,000	2,096	.182696	383	1,367	164	1,914
1981	10,000	2,096	.204619	429	1,914	230	2,573
1982	10,000	2,096	.229174	480	2,573	309	3,362
1983	10,000	2,096	.256675	538	3,362	404	4,304
1984	10,000	2,096	.287476	603	4,304	516	5,423
1985	10,000	2,096	.321973	675	5,423	651	6,749
1986	10,000	2,096	.360610	755	6,749	810	8,314
1987	10,000	2,096	.403883	847	8,314	998	10,159
1988	10,000	2,096	.452349	948	10,159	1,219	12,326
1989	10,000	2,096	.506631	1,062	12,326	1,479	14,867
1990	10,000	2,096	.567426	1,189	14,867	1,784	17,840
1991	10,000	2,096	.635518	1,332	17,840	2,141	21,313
1992	10,000	2,096	.711780	1,492	21,313	2,557	25,362
1993	10,000	2,096	.797193	1,671	25,362	3,043	30,076
1994	10,000	2,096	.892857	1,871	30,076	3,609	35,556
1995	10,000	2,096	1.000000	2,096	35,556	4,267	41,919
	$200,000						

* Percentage of (a) the present value of estimated pension benefits at December 31, 1995, to (b) total compensation to December 31, 1995—$41,919 ÷ $200,000 = 20.9595%.

Assumptions for Table 3

Hired—January 1, 1976
Retirement date—December 31, 1995
Discount rate, including an allowance both for an interest factor
  and for population decrements—12%

Present value at retirement date of estimated pension benefits:
  Base—average earnings for final three years prior
    to retirement $10,000
  Annual pension—50% of base   5,000
  Present value at retirement date, at 6%, assuming
    benefits will be paid at the end of each year for
    12 years subsequent to the retirement date
    ($5,000 × 8.38384394) 41,919

In this illustration where annual compensation is assumed to remain level (Column 2), the pension benefits assigned to each year
(Column 3) also remain level. Because each year's assigned benefits
are then discounted to present value, however, the accrual (Column
5) increases (both in absolute terms and as a percentage of salary)
throughout the period of employment.

As with the cost-correlation method, we shall also illustrate how
the benefit-correlation method is applied to a more realistic situation
in which compensation increases throughout the participant's employment. Table 4 employs the same assumptions as were used in
Table 2.

Assumptions for Table 4

Hired—January 1, 1976
Retirement date—December 31, 1995
Compensation increase—8% annually compounded (includes in-
  creases assumed to result from inflation)
Discount rate, including an allowance both for an interest factor
  and for population decrements—12%
Present value at retirement date of estimated pension benefits:

  Base—average earnings for final three years prior
    to retirement .... $ 40,039
  Annual pension—50% of base   20,020
  Present value at retirement date, at 6%, assuming
    benefits will be paid at the end of each year for

TABLE 4

Illustration of Pension Accrual for a Single Participant Derived by Correlating the Pension Benefits with Compensation (assuming increasing compensation)

(1)	(2)	(3)	(4)	(5)	(6)	(7)	(8)
		Correlation of Pension Benefit with Compensation	Present Value	Accrual Based on Present Value of	Accrued Obligation		
Year	Annual Compensation	(2) × 36.6780%*	of $1 Payable at Retirement	Pension Benefits (3) × (4)	Beginning of Year	Discount Rate Applied to Beginning Balance	End of Year (5) + (6) + (7)
1976	$ 10,000	$ 3,668	.116106	$ 426	$ —	$ —	$ 426
1977	10,800	3,961	.130039	515	426	51	992
1978	11,664	4,278	.145644	623	992	119	1,734
1979	12,597	4,620	.163121	754	1,734	208	2,696
1980	13,605	4,990	.182696	912	2,696	324	3,932
1981	14,693	5,389	.204619	1,103	3,932	472	5,507
1982	15,869	5,820	.229174	1,334	5,507	660	7,501
1983	17,138	6,286	.256675	1,613	7,501	900	10,014
1984	18,509	6,789	.287476	1,952	10,014	1,201	13,167
1985	19,990	7,332	.321973	2,361	13,167	1,580	17,108
1986	21,589	7,918	.360610	2,855	17,108	2,053	22,016
1987	23,316	8,552	.403883	3,454	22,016	2,642	28,112
1988	25,182	9,236	.452349	4,178	28,112	3,373	35,663
1989	27,196	9,975	.506631	5,054	35,663	4,279	44,996
1990	29,372	10,773	.567426	6,113	44,996	5,399	56,508
1991	31,722	11,635	.635518	7,394	56,508	6,781	70,683
1992	34,259	12,565	.711780	8,944	70,683	8,482	88,109
1993	37,000	13,571	.797193	10,819	88,109	10,573	109,501
1994	39,960	14,656	.892857	13,086	109,501	13,141	135,728
1995	43,157	15,829	1.000000	15,829	135,728	16,288	167,845
	$457,618						

* Percentage of (a) the present value of estimated pension benefits at December 31, 1995, to (b) total compensation to December 31, 1995—$167,845 ÷ $457,618 = 36.6780%.

12 years subsequent to the retirement date
($20,020 × 8.38384394) $167,845

Although less apparent, the same relationships exist as in Table 3. First, the assigned benefits for each year (Column 3) are a constant percentage of annual compensation (Column 2) throughout the period of employment—hence the term "benefit-correlation." Second, because of the present value factors applied, the accrual of the pension obligation (Column 5) increases each year, not only in absolute amounts but also as a percentage of compensation.

COMPARATIVE ANALYSIS OF TWO METHODS

As has been illustrated in the preceding Tables 1–4, the pattern for the accrual of the obligation for pension benefits based on employee performance as measured by compensation differs significantly depending upon whether such accrual is based upon a cost-correlation or benefit-correlation approach. The differing results are summarized from Tables 1–4 as shown in Tables 5 and 6.

TABLE 5

Comparison of Pension Accrual Patterns Derived under the Cost-Correlation and Benefit-Correlation Methods (assuming level compensation)

	Cost-Correlation Method			Benefit-Correlation Method		
	Accrual		Liability	Accrual		Liability
	On Com-		End	On Com-		End
Year	pensation	Interest	of Year	pensation	Interest	of Year
1976	$581	$ —	$ 581	$ 243	$ —	$ 243
1977	581	69	1,231	273	29	545
1978	581	148	1,960	305	65	915
1979	581	236	2,777	342	110	1,367
1980	581	334	3,692	383	164	1,914
1981	581	444	4,717	429	230	2,573
1982	581	567	5,865	480	309	3,362
1983	581	705	7,151	538	404	4,304
1984	581	859	8,591	603	516	5,423
1985	581	1,032	10,204	675	651	6,749
1986	581	1,226	12,011	755	810	8,314
1987	581	1,443	14,035	847	998	10,159
1988	581	1,686	16,302	948	1,219	12,326
1989	581	1,958	18,841	1,062	1,479	14,867
1990	581	2,263	21,685	1,189	1,784	17,840
1991	581	2,604	24,870	1,332	2,141	21,313
1992	581	2,986	28,437	1,492	2,557	25,362
1993	581	3,414	32,432	1,671	3,043	30,076
1994	581	3,894	36,907	1,871	3,609	35,556
1995	581	4,431	41,919	2,096	4,267	41,919

The cost-correlation method probably has an immediate appeal to many accountants. Imbued as they are with the matching concept and an almost instinctive preference for any accrual technique that tends to smooth expenses, accountants would generally opt for a method that results in an accrual that maintains a constant relationship to direct compensation. Furthermore, the cost-correlation method results in a faster accrual of the liability—a conservatism that accountants traditionally look on with favor.

Arguments in favor of the cost-correlation method are not limited,

TABLE 6

Comparison of Pension Accrual Patterns Derived under the Cost-Correlation and Benefit-Correlation Methods (assuming increasing compensation)

	Cost-Correlation Method			Benefit-Correlation Method		
	Accrual		Liability	Accrual		Liability
Year	On Compensation	Interest	End of Year	On Compensation	Interest	End of Year
1976	$1,347	$ —	$ 1,347	$ 426	$ —	$ 426
1977	1,454	162	2,963	515	51	992
1978	1,571	356	4,890	623	119	1,734
1979	1,696	587	7,173	754	208	2,696
1980	1,832	861	9,866	912	324	3,932
1981	1,979	1,184	13,029	1,103	472	5,507
1982	2,137	1,562	16,728	1,334	660	7,501
1983	2,308	2,007	21,043	1,613	900	10,014
1984	2,493	2,525	26,061	1,952	1,201	13,167
1985	2,692	3,127	31,880	2,361	1,580	17,108
1986	2,907	3,826	38,613	2,855	2,053	22,016
1987	3,140	4,634	46,387	3,454	2,642	28,112
1988	3,391	5,566	55,344	4,178	3,373	35,663
1989	3,663	6,641	65,648	5,054	4,279	44,996
1990	3,956	7,878	77,482	6,113	5,399	56,508
1991	4,272	9,298	91,052	7,394	6,781	70,683
1992	4,614	10,927	106,593	8,944	8,482	88,109
1993	4,983	12,791	124,367	10,819	10,573	109,501
1994	5,381	14,924	144,672	13,086	13,141	135,728
1995	5,812	17,361	167,845	15,829	16,288	167,845

however, to a superficial preference for the result. Many accounting accruals employ some form of straight-line allocation among periods. It can also be argued that, since pensions are a portion of employees' overall compensation, the entire compensation cost should be accrued on a consistent basis, with direct compensation establishing the pattern.

We have concluded, however, that the benefit-correlation method best reflects the objectives of financial statements that we have adopted and discussed earlier in this monograph. These objectives reject the matching approach, with its overemphasis on the income statement. Conservatism, in and of itself, should not be a goal. Rather, the approach should be to measure economic resources and obligations, with changes from period to period (other than those of a capital nature) constituting net income or loss.

The cost-correlation method is what its name implies. It results in an assignment to each period of what is assumed to be the appropriate cost. The accrued pension liability at the end of any period is the by-product of this cost-oriented approach. A sound conceptual support for the resulting year-end liability cannot be developed for this approach, however, as it focuses solely on an income-statement cost-allocation technique.

The benefit-correlation method, on the other hand, starts with a measure, year by year, of the ending pension obligation applicable to each year. In effect, each year's accrual based on compensation represents the amount that would be required to purchase an annuity payable on retirement for benefits earned that year on the basis of direct compensation. Similarly, the pension liability at any year end approximates the amount that would be required to purchase an annuity for pension benefits earned to date. There could not be a more economically substantive measure of the obligation that accrues each year and accumulates at each year end.

The contrasting results between the cost-correlation and the benefit-correlation methods and the propriety of adopting the latter approach can be demonstrated even more simply, perhaps, in the following illustration. Let us assume an employee aged 55 is promised a lump sum payment of $100,000 when he retires at age 65. We shall ignore for this illustration the complexity of correlating the accrual with compensation because compensation is the basis for both of the accrual methods under consideration and because we have already discussed why the pension obligation should, in our view, be recorded as employee performance, measured by compensation, takes place. We might consider accruing the liability that arises under the above assumptions either by—

Determining an accrual based on level payments that would be required each year to provide a benefit that would aggregate $100,000 at retirement, or

Determining an accrual based on the amount that would be required each year to provide $10,000 (one-tenth of the total benefit) payable at retirement.

TABLE 7

Alternative Methods of Accruing for a $100,000 Liability Due in Ten Years

(1)	(2)	(3)	(4)	(5)	(6)	(7)
	Level Annual Payments			Level Benefit Purchase		
		Interest at 6% on		Amount to Provide—		
	Amount	Beginning	End-of-Year	1/10 of	Interest	End-of-Year
Year	Deposited	Balance	Balance	$100,000	at 6%	Balance
1........	$ 7,587	$ —	$ 7,587	$ 5,919	$ —	$ 5,919
2........	7,587	455	15,629	6,274	355	12,548
3........	7,587	938	24,154	6,651	753	19,952
4........	7,587	1,449	33,190	7,050	1,197	28,199
5........	7,587	1,991	42,768	7,473	1,692	37,364
6........	7,587	2,566	52,921	7,921	2,242	47,527
7........	7,587	3,175	63,683	8,396	2,852	58,775
8........	7,587	3,821	75,091	8,900	3,526	71,201
9........	7,587	4,505	87,183	9,434	4,272	84,907
10........	7,587	5,230	100,000	10,000	5,093	100,000
	$75,870			$78,018		

These methods are illustrated in Table 7.

It probably does not require pointing out that the level-payments approach shown in Columns 2–4 is the same as the cost-correlation method and that the level-benefit approach shown in Columns 5–7 is the same as the benefit-correlation method. In this example, it is clearly demonstrated that the benefit-correlation method is based on measurement of the liability since annual payments of the amounts shown in Column 5 would be the amounts required to liquidate each year's share of the total obligation for benefits (and the same would be true with respect to the end-of-year balance). On the other hand, the accrued obligation in Column 4 that results under the cost-correlation method can be explained only in terms of the computation from which it is derived—it has no sound conceptual definition.

It must be emphasized that our conclusions with respect to the appropriate method for accruing pension obligations are based solely on accounting considerations. We recognize that other methods, specifically including the cost-correlation method discussed above, are widely used by actuaries in establishing pension funding programs; and we do not question their appropriateness. The considerations that go into funding decisions may sometimes parallel accounting considerations, but this is not necessarily (or perhaps frequently) the case. Such differences, after all, are what distinguish accrual from cash-basis accounting.

chapter 7

Accounting for Pension Costs by Sponsoring Employers

THE PRINCIPLES that now govern accounting for pension costs by the employer are set forth in *APB Opinion No. 8*. Although the approach that we recommend differs from *Opinion No. 8* in many important respects, we believe that the FASB could issue a financial accounting standard on accounting for pension costs that would incorporate most of our basic proposals without changing the general framework of present accounting practices. This is generally true even if the standard that the FASB issues with respect to accounting for pension plans as separate reporting entities should differ in certain respects from our recommendations. As we shall point out, however, action on one of our recommendations would probably have to be deferred until such time as financial statement objectives along the general lines we advocate are accepted.

The first part of this chapter deals with the accounting for pension costs by an employer sponsoring a defined benefit type of pension plan. As indicated in Chapter 5, under such a plan the benefits to be paid to participating employees upon retirement are fixed, and it is the employer (rather than the employee) who assumes the risks to meet the obligation for payment of such benefits. The ultimate obligation of the employer is subject to many variables, the effect of which must be estimated.

In the latter part of this chapter, we shall comment on defined contribution and certain insured plans, the accounting for which is simplified because the risk of payment of a defined future benefit is not assumed by the employer.

COMPARISON OF FINANCIAL STATEMENT OBJECTIVES
WITH PENSION FUNDING OBJECTIVES

In developing the accounting principles that most accurately communicate the economic substance of pension-related transactions, it is important that the objectives of financial statements be differentiated from the objectives of pension funding. Much confusion has arisen in previous attempts to formulate accounting principles in this area because these differing objectives have not properly been recognized.

When developing a plan for funding pension benefits, it is, of course, important to estimate the requirements for funds ultimately to be needed to meet the related pension obligations. A strategy for discharging this obligation is a form of budgeting of the future use of resources. The long-term nature of pension costs should be considered. Stability in the year-to-year requirements for funds to meet the obligation may be a proper goal. In order to protect against unanticipated future cash shortages, a conservative policy that results in accelerated funding in earlier years may be prudent. Any one of several actuarial methods may be considered to meet this funding objective.

The objectives of financial statements, however, differ from those of funding. Financial statements purport to communicate the financial position as of a specified date, and the results of operations from period to period. The long-term nature of pension costs is not a relevant characteristic that should be considered in communicating the value of economic resources and the interest of creditors and equity owners in such resources at a specified date. Although accounting principles should assume the continuing existence of the business enterprise in the absence of evidence to the contrary, and although the cost of providing pension benefits is a continuing one, investors need to know the financial status of a business enterprise as of a particular point in time. They need to make economic decisions periodically and require information regarding the currently existing values and obligations of the business enterprise in order to make such economic decisions effectively.

CONSISTENCY BETWEEN PLAN AND EMPLOYER
ACCOUNTING FOR PENSIONS

The FASB *Discussion Memorandum*, "Accounting and Reporting for Employee Benefit Plans," noted that consideration of the need, if any, for consistency between plan and employer accounting fell outside its scope but that this issue would be considered specifically in the project, "Accounting for the Cost of Pension Plans." The *Discussion Memorandum* went on to point out, however, that this issue of employer/plan symmetry and its implications should not be overlooked by respondents to the *Discussion Memorandum* dealing with the plan.[1]

If our views on accounting for pension plans are accepted, we believe that employer/plan symmetry is appropriate and should be followed in the accounting for pension costs. Such symmetry becomes necessary because the pension plan as a separate entity lacks economic substance apart from that of the employer.

Looking through the form to the economic substance of pension plan arrangements, we do not believe that the obligation for pension benefits can logically be considered a liability of the plan unless it is considered as, first, a liability of the sponsoring employer. The plan is merely a vehicle for discharging the responsibilities an employer has undertaken to provide pension benefits to its employees. It is the employees' services *to the employer* that provide the basis for recognizing and measuring the liability for pension benefits. The plan's liability would be a hollow one indeed if it were not backed by the resources and the obligations of the employer.

In reaching the conclusion that symmetry is appropriate, we have been influenced primarily by our concept of the nature of a liability, as discussed generally in Chapter 3 and as applied to plan pension obligations in Chapters 5 and 6. Liabilities represent claims against the economic resources of an entity. This recognition of liabilities should be based on substantive (even though not necessarily legally binding) claims, some of which accrue with the passage of time or upon the occurrence of certain measurable events. With respect to pension plans, a liability is incurred by the employer as performance is completed by the employees.

Stated otherwise, the employer has assumed an obligation for pension benefits and will be required to pay amounts in satisfaction of that obligation during some future periods. To the extent that the obligation to make future payment relates to services already rendered by the employees, a liability has been incurred and should be recorded in the financial statements of the employer.

Some have relied upon legal concepts in contending that the liability for pension benefits need not be recognized by the employer

[1] FASB, *Discussion Memorandum* (Stamford, Conn., 1975), see particularly pp. 3–5.

until the liability is funded through contributions to the pension trust. They argue that the trust serves to insulate the employer from the legal liability. We do not believe that such an argument is valid from an economic point of view, and evolutionary changes in the pension environment support our contention. The enactment of ERISA serves as a recent illustration of such changes. Although ERISA may not have resulted in the addition of any legal responsibility for business enterprises to provide benefits for their retired employees, its provisions do serve to add weight to the economic as opposed to the legal view of the pension liability. Minimum funding and vesting requirements, as well as termination guarantee provisions contained in ERISA, serve to reduce this insulation. Because the employer is now required ultimately to fund those benefits defined in the plan, its obligation to provide the promised retirement benefits becomes more direct. Future payments required by the employer with respect to benefits earned to date represent a present liability.

As noted in Chapter 2, the FASB through the issuance of *Interpretation No. 3*, has concluded that ERISA does not create a legal obligation for unfunded pension costs that warrants recognition as a liability pursuant to *APB Opinion No. 8*, except under specified (but not common) circumstances.[2] We do not disagree with this *Interpretation*, but our rationale for requiring a sponsoring employer to recognize a liability for its obligation for pension benefits is not predicated upon such legal determinations.

As indicated in the FASB *Discussion Memorandum*, there are three approaches to employer/plan symmetry, as follows:

> [1] The accounts of the plan might be included in the financial statements of the employer, much in the same way as a subsidiary is consolidated in the financial statements of the parent company. . . .
>
> [2] The employer might be required to treat the unfunded obligation for plan benefits in a manner that is analogous to the accounting for investments by the equity method; only the obligation net of plan assets would be presented. . . .
>
> [3] Even if the plan's assets and liabilities are not directly incorporated in the employer's financial statements, the concept of symmetry, if adopted, might have an effect on accounting for the cost of pension plans. Periodic pension cost presently is based on

---

[2] FASB, *Interpretation No. 3* (Stamford, Conn., 1974).

both a measure of the plan obligations and measures of the assets available to satisfy those obligations. Thus, if employer/plan accounting symmetry were applied in any future pronouncement of the FASB, the asset and liability measurement issues set forth in this Discussion Memorandum might affect the measurement of pension cost by the employer.[3]

We do not disagree with the idea embodied in alternative 3 above that symmetry includes a consistency in measurement principles, and our financial statement objectives strive for such consistency in the measurement of assets and liabilities for any reporting entity. However, our conclusions set forth above with respect to (a) the lack of separate economic substance of the pension plan, and (b) the assumption by the employer of the substantive pension liability lead to a more direct concept of symmetry that includes the incorporation of the plan's fund balance (or deficit) into the accounts of the employer's financial statements.

In our view, the employer/plan symmetry is most properly reflected by the adoption of the approach suggested by alternative 2 in the *FASB Discussion Memorandum* (i.e., the equity method analogy), rather than alternative 1 calling for full consolidation of the plan's assets and liabilities. Consolidation is questionable because the employer does not have the same control over the assets and liabilities of the pension plan as he does those of a subsidiary company. Most evident in this regard is the fact that the plan's funded assets are not available to, nor may they inure to the benefit of the employer—except to satisfy the employer's obligation under the plan. From the employer's viewpoint the economic substance of the pension plan transactions is best reported by reflecting the obligation for pension benefits net of the value of the funded assets of the plan available for satisfaction of the obligation.

To reflect the assets and liabilities of the plan in the financial statements of the employer in a manner analogous to the adoption of the equity method (alternative No. 2 in the *Discussion Memorandum*) properly considers the fact that the employer has assumed the pension obligation and is bearing the risks associated with the ownership of the plan's funded assets available to meet that obligation. As we note later in this chapter, disclosure of the condensed financial statements of a single-employer plan in a note to the financial statements of the employer is also appropriate.

---

[3] FASB, *Discussion Memorandum*, p. 4.

It follows, then, that the employer should record as a liability the unfunded obligation of the plan—i.e., the plan's liabilities (primarily for pension benefits) less the current value of the plan's assets resulting from the accumulated contributions and the accumulated plan earnings (net of benefit distributions). The unfunded obligation of the plan that provides the basis for the employer's liability must result from an appropriate determination of plan obligations for benefits earned to date by the employees calculated in accordance with the criteria described in Chapters 5 and 6. Where the current value of the plan's assets exceeds the plan's liability for pension benefits earned to date, the resulting fund balance would be an asset of the employer, representing the advance funding or prepayment of the pension obligation to be earned in future periods by the employees.

If we were to assume that (a) there were no obligations for services rendered by employees prior to the adoption or amendment of a plan, and (b) there were no actuarial gains or losses occurring during the period (admittedly oversimplified assumptions used for the purpose of illustration only), and if the employer were to fund its pension obligation currently, then the following would result under our proposal:

There would be no liability (or asset) for pension costs reflected in the employer's balance sheet.

The amount paid to the plan to fund its pension obligation would be equal to the provision for pension costs for the period.

The "ideal" situation, however, does not exist in practice. The accounting becomes more complex, and probably more controversial, because (a) there are past-service obligations that arise when the plan is adopted or amended and (b) actuarial gains and losses are bound to arise. In addition, the employer's funding of the plan often does not follow the same pattern as the increase in the plan's unfunded obligation. The effects of these complexities are discussed in the sections that follow.

TREATMENT OF CONTRA TO THE LIABILITY
FOR THE PAST-SERVICE OBLIGATION

Although we have considered it necessary to support our views that the unfunded obligation for pension benefits is a liability of the sponsoring employer by initially discussing pension plan accounting in some detail and then developing the case for employer/plan symmetry ,we suspect that most accountants and others either come to or are faced with this conclusion almost intuitively. Some have tried to "wish it away," but it is an inescapable fact that persistently rears its head.

To the extent that such an unfunded obligation arises out of a discretionary decision not to fund current or "normal" costs as such costs are determined under a company's actuarial method, practice has properly been to accrue a liability, with an offsetting debit to expense. Under existing practice, the "normal" costs can be computed using any one of several actuarial methods, whereas we believe that there is only one proper way to measure such "normal" costs—that is, as earned through performance by employees, measured as described in Chapter 6.

With respect to the portion of the obligation that relates to service performed by employees prior to the date when a plan is adopted or amended, however, a special problem arises. Accountants have avoided the term "past-service liability"; instead, they have resorted to the euphemism "past-service cost." Except where current costs have not been funded as discussed in the preceding paragraph, use of the term "liability" in connection with pension past-service costs is generally restricted in authoritative accounting pronouncements to the narrow area of legal liabilities, which is somewhat inconsistent with accountants' willingness to recognize other substantive accrued liabilities (e.g., warranties) without concern as to whether they are legally binding.

We are convinced that this avoidance of acknowledging as a liability what actuaries and many others refer to as a liability or an obligation stems from a recognition that putting a liability for unfunded past-service costs on the employer's balance sheet creates an offsetting debit that must be accounted for. If this debit would always be small, no one would probably have been concerned about writing it off or carrying it as a deferred charge. Since it might frequently amount to millions—even hundreds of millions—of dollars, however, accountants have historically ignored the embarrassing debit by decreeing that there is no liability.

Because we have concluded, however, that a substantive liability does exist, and must be recognized by employers, for unfunded pension obligations, it is necessary to decide how the debit should be handled for that portion of the unfunded pension obligation that represents a liability for past service. We shall consider this, first, within the general framework of existing practice (i.e., how the debit should be handled under current "matching" concepts) and, second, in accordance with our view of financial statement objectives (i.e., how the debit should be treated if the general framework were changed in accordance with the objectives we have identified).

Under Current "Matching" Concepts

There is no question that employers, when they establish, revise, or negotiate with employees regarding pension plans, consider the entire cost of the plans to be an element of compensation for present and future services of their employees. Sometimes there are trade-offs between direct compensation and pension benefits. Certainly no employers today believe that they establish or supplement pension plans as rewards for past services any more than they believe that increased salaries and wages granted relate directly to past services. Decisions with respect to pension plans are forward looking.

As noted in Chapter 3, much of today's accounting is based on a "matching" concept, this concept provides that expenses should be matched with revenues—that is, they should be recorded in those periods in which the related revenues are recognized. Under this prevalent matching concept, we believe that it can be argued today that the debit offsetting that portion of the liability for unfunded pension obligations that represents past-service costs should be set up as a deferred charge and amortized by charges to income of future periods, responsive to the "forward looking" impact of the pension negotiation. Until such time as the underlying concepts with respect to financial statements might be changed to reflect our recommendations (as discussed in the section immediately following), we would accept this approach.

The periods over which the deferred charges should be amortized should be the anticipated period of remaining service of present employees at the time a plan is adopted or amended. The pattern of amortization should be similar to that for accrual of plan obligations as discussed in Chapters 5 and 6.

One might ask why this change is necessary—why it is necessary to record the past-service cost as a liability if the related charge is to be deferred and amortized. There are three answers.

First, there *is* a liability; and sound accounting (either under our objectives or under present-day practice) requires accounting recognition of a liability without regard to how the contra debit is treated.

Second, setting up the deferred charge and amortizing it on the basis described above provides a more direct and better "matching" with the related services than does the arbitrary, yet flexible, amortization of past-service costs permitted under APB Opinion No. 8.

Third and possibly most important, setting up the deferred charge properly discloses, on the face of the balance sheet, the present value of costs related to past service that must be borne by future periods. The conclusion is inescapable that managements, employees, and the public frequently fail to recognize the imbedded cost for past service that often arises when pension plans are amended. This is particularly true with respect to public bodies.

When neither the liability for past service nor the related cost is reflected in the balance sheet, these amounts are easy to overlook. Sometimes past-service costs are not even disclosed; and the vastly differing determinations under various accepted actuarial methods (some of which do not even identify a past-service amount) render even those disclosures that are made meaningless. It is easy to pile one amendment to a pension plan on top of another with ever increasing benefits when the present value of the cost of such benefits is not reflected in the employer's financial statements.

Our method would recognize a liability for past service that is attributable to the portion of the estimated pension benefits that has been earned by employees through performance prior to the time when the plan (or plan amendment) was adopted, measured as discussed in Chapter 6. The adoption of our proposal would eliminate the vastly differing determinations of past-service costs that exist under the various actuarial methods now acceptable under APB Opinion No. 8.

Some readers may express a concern that reflecting the liability and, particularly, the debit for past-service costs in the financial statements might put a damper on the willingness of companies to adopt pension plans or to grant more liberal benefits through plan amendments. Although we can understand the concern, we do not consider it relevant to a determination regarding the manner of accounting for plan adoptions or amendments. The function of accounting is to present reliable and impartial information—not to add, withhold or take editorial liberties with the facts because the preparer wishes to cause or to prevent some action that might otherwise result.

It is only because we have noted this reasoning in other situations that we raise the point. In discussions on accounting for the effects of inflation, for example, some persons have expressed concern that showing the impact would fuel further inflation by making apparent the need for price increases. Similarly in the area of accounting for leases, it has frequently been asserted that showing a lease obligation on a lessee's balance sheet would adversely affect the lessee's credit rating. Such arguments have no place in the establishment of sound accounting standards.

Under Our Concept of Financial Statement Objectives

Although we have concluded in the immediately preceding section that deferral and amortization (on a rational basis) of past-service costs that arise when a plan is adopted or amended are acceptable under current matching concepts, it is obvious that this conclusion is not in accordance with the objectives of financial statements that we have advocated in Chapter 3. Such accounting reflects those outmoded and misleading concepts that, in our view, have created much of today's disillusionment with financial accounting and reporting. It has been asserted that the matching concept has frequently resulted in the matching of soft assets against hard liabilities in the balance sheet. This is the result that emerges from application of the procedures set forth in the preceding section.

To restate and summarize from the financial statement objectives we proposed in Chapter 3, it is our view that:

1.   Only economic resources that possess the characteristics of utility, scarcity and exchangeability should be recognized as assets.
2.   Changes in net economic resources (except as they result from capital transactions) should be reflected in the income statement as they occur.

From this, it follows that we do not consider the debit arising from recognition of the liability for past-service costs to be a valid asset that should be reported as such in an employer's balance sheet. It is not exchangeable—that is, it does not have a characteristic that allows it to be sold or exchanged for other assets, or used to satisfy a claim by a creditor. It is not an economic resource that is separable from the business as a whole. Accordingly, if our views regarding the objectives of financial statements were to be adopted, such a debit related to past service should be included in the income statement for the period in which a pension plan is adopted or amended.

Rationale for Not Deferring Past-Service Costs

This does not imply that the costs of past-service pension benefits relate to the prior years (when the services on which the determination is based were provided) nor that they lack value. The decision to credit employees with benefits for past service may be of great value in terms of present and future employer/employee relations and employee morale. It may even be essential to the company's continuing operations. But such value is not separable from the business as a whole; it is solely dependent upon the business enterprise to which the pension costs are attached.

The accounting profession appears to be, and we hope is, moving toward expensing intangibles rather than treating them as assets in the vague category of deferred charges. A case in point is accounting for research and development costs. In October 1974, the FASB concluded that research and development costs should be charged to expense as incurred and should not be capitalized as deferred charges and amortized in future periods.[4] The FASB reached this conclusion not on the basis that the expenditures were without value or would not benefit future periods but, rather, because future benefits, although possibly foreseen, "cannot be measured with a reasonable degree of certainty."[5] As is true with research and development costs, there is no perceptible relationship between past-service pension costs incurred, and the related value attributable to any future period.

In summary, we acknowledge that pension plans are negotiated by employers using a "forward looking" point of view. In this sense, pension transactions are no different from research and development activities and many other transactions entered into by business enterprises. But the forward looking nature of such transactions does not necessarily allow for all the associated costs to be recorded as assets and "matched" against future operations. When no economic re-

---

[4] Financial Accounting Standards Board, "Accounting for Research and Development Costs," *Statement of Financial Accounting Standards No. 2*, (Stamford, Conn., 1974).

[5] Ibid., paragraph 45. The FASB reached its conclusion on the basis of measurability of future economic benefits and neither accepted nor rejected at that time (or since) our other criterion, exchangeability, as a criterion for accounting recognition of an economic resource.

source having a value apart from the value of the business as a whole arises from the transaction, financial statement users are best served if the related costs are immediately recognized as an expense of the period. Only with this treatment will financial statements properly communicate the economic resources of the enterprise and the changes in such resources in the periods in which they occur.

Treatment of Past-Service Costs in the Income Statement

At this juncture, some readers, while not necessarily disagreeing with our views regarding the nature of assets, may object to charging the entire past-service cost immediately to expense on the basis either that this charge distorts income or that it is not related to the period's operations. Regarding the first point, distortion, like beauty, is in the eye of the beholder. What is distortion to one person may be "telling it like it is" to another. The distortion criticism is based on an assumption that some kind of "smoothed income" is the norm. Some who hold this view cite the "long-range nature" of pension costs as a justification, but, as explained earlier, such a view erroneously confuses the long-term nature of pension *funding* with the financial statement objectives of communicating the value of economic resources as of a specified date. We believe, and hope, that accountants are abandoning the false goal inherent in the desires for "smoothed income."

We have more sympathy for the second concern stated above— that the charge for past-service costs is not related to current operations. For years, relevance to current operations was the criterion many, if not most, accountants applied in determining what items should enter the determination of net income. Ten years of a steadily changing concept of income, starting with *APB Opinion No. 9*[6] in 1966 and reinforced with a series of subsequent APB Opinions and FASB Statements, have not completely eliminated that view—nor is the view without continuing merit.

The problem is that, in spite of the increasing emphasis on the inclusion (but segregation) of extraordinary items in income, we still have not satisfactorily solved the problems of what the income statement should include or how the components should be classified and presented. In fact, the existing criteria for extraordinary items, as

[6] American Institute of Certified Public Accountants, "Reporting the Results of Operations," *APB Opinion No. 9* (New York, 1966).

set forth mainly in *APB Opinion No. 30*,[7] have been such as to eliminate, rather than clarify, the distinction between operating items and other items of income and expense (almost everything is now operations).

As discussed in Chapter 3, it is our view that the present form of income statement should be substantially revised. Although the form we recommend is based on our concept of the objectives of financial statements, much of what we recommend could well be adopted within the framework of present accounting practices. In summary, we believe that the income statement should include the following categories, to the extent applicable, with appropriate detail within each category:

Operating earnings.

Financial expenses.

Charges for intangibles.

Provision for income taxes.

Unusual items not relevant to an assessment
of continuing operating earnings.

Nonoperating holding gains or losses.

Provision for maintenance of capital.

With such a form of income statement, there would be less need for concern whether items of income or expense reported during the period are related to current operations. Elements that are substantially different in their character would not be jumbled together as they are under existing income statement formats. This form of income statement should lead to a different and more informed use by readers. The "bottom line" would no longer be so all important. Less emphasis would be placed on the overly simplistic per-share amount. Amounts reported could be evaluated more readily in terms of their nature. Current operating earnings would be more readily distinguishable from the other elements which contribute to the change in net economic resources from period to period.

With this form of income statement, we envision no problem of readers being misled by charging the initial cost of past service incurred when a pension plan is adopted or amended to the "charges

---

[7] American Institute of Certified Public Accountants, "Reporting the Results of Operations," *APB Opinion No. 30* (New York, 1973).

for intangibles" category while charging costs related to current service to operating earnings.[8]

TREATMENT OF ACTUARIAL GAINS OR LOSSES

Consistent with our concept of the objectives of financial statements, actuarial gains or losses, including realized and unrealized gains or losses in the current value of plan assets, should be included in current income. Under a defined benefit plan, since (a) the risk of ownership of plan assets runs to the employer, and (b) the obligation of the plan is a substantive liability of the employer, the changes in these amounts (including those changes that are characterized as actuarial gains and losses) contribute to the changes in the net economic resources of the employer. Consequently, they should be reflected as they occur in the financial statements of the employer.

As discussed in Chapter 5, some contend that valuation of plan assets at current value is not compatible with actuarial valuations of pension obligations. Such actuarial methods typically involve a spreading of actuarial and investment gains and losses and employ interest assumptions different from those implicit in valuing fixed income securities at market. Such apparent inconsistencies are reconciled when the differing objectives of financial reporting and pension funding are considered. The current value approach should be used to measure an entity's financial position *at a single point in time*—to measure its resources at that point in time, and the extent to which these resources compare with its obligations. On the other hand, actuarial techniques are used to project total pension benefits *over a period of time*, and the funding required during that period to meet the estimated obligations. The concepts of spreading gains and losses and making long-term interest and other actuarial assumptions (which may differ from circumstances as of a particular date) are valid when estimating what will occur over a future period of time, but such concepts are not relevant to a measure of actual resources as of a particular date.

---

[8] Although we have recommended a single, multisection form of income statement as described in this monograph, we do not reject the possibility that the various categories might be further segregated into two or more separate statements that, taken together, would set forth a period's change in shareholders' investment (exclusive of capital additions and distributions). Because of the differences in nature of the categories (and the resulting differences in users' appraisal of their significance), a persuasive argument can be advanced for not putting them in a single statement coming to a total called "net income."

To the extent that gains or losses on investments over and above those assumed as part of the actuarial interest rate assumption, whether realized or unrealized, enter into changes in the plan's unfunded obligation for the year, the amount of such gains or losses should be included (but separately identified) under the caption "Nonoperating holding gains or losses" in the company's income statement.

INCOME TAX EFFECTS

The accounting for pension costs that we recommend would result in differences between income for financial reporting purposes and income determined for tax purposes. Such a situation is not uncommon today; there are many such differences, including ones that may result from present practices in accounting for pension costs. APB *Opinion No. 8* recognized and provided for this type of situation as follows:

> When pension cost is recognized for tax purposes in a period other than the one in which recognized for financial reporting purposes, appropriate consideration should be given to allocation of income taxes among accounting periods.[9]

We consider such tax allocation (sometimes referred to as "deferred tax" accounting), which was affirmed in general terms in *APB Opinion No. 11*, "Accounting for Income Taxes,"[10] to be appropriate under both existing and our proposed standards.

FINANCIAL STATEMENT DISCLOSURES

The adoption of our recommendations regarding the accounting by sponsoring employers for the cost of pension plans would result in the elimination of some of the financial statement disclosure requirements presently existing under *APB Opinion No. 8* and SEC *Regulation S–X*. The elimination of equally acceptable accounting alternatives would allow for the elimination of the disclosure of the description of the accounting method used. In addition, the financial statement recognition of past-service costs would make disclosure of

---

[9] AICPA, *APB Opinion No. 8*, paragraph 45.

[10] American Institute of Certified Public Accountants, "Accounting for Income Taxes," *APB Opinion No. 11* (New York, 1967).

the amounts and, if our complete recommendations were adopted, amortization periods with respect to such costs no longer relevant. The remaining disclosures now required under *APB Opinion No. 8* (see Chapter 2) would continue to be appropriate.

We recommend that additional disclosures be included in the notes to the financial statements of the sponsoring employer summarizing the condensed financial position of a single-employer plan. Such disclosures would inform the financial statement reader of the total obligation for pension benefits earned to date by the employees and the nature and amount of the plan's funded assets that can be used in satisfaction of this obligation. Although the funded assets are restricted and normally may be utilized only in satisfaction of the employer's pension obligation, disclosure of the amount of such assets, together with a description as to their nature, is pertinent because the employer assumes the risk of ownership of such assets. For this reason, a brief description of the pension plans' investment policies would also be meaningful.

DEFINED CONTRIBUTION AND INSURED PLANS

The differing economic characteristics of defined contribution plans and insured plans result in differing accounting principles. With respect to a defined contribution pension plan, employer contributions are usually required in accordance with stated plan provisions, and benefits are based upon the accumulation of the funds generated by such contributions together with the earnings (losses) attributable to these funds. As indicated previously, the risks of ownership of the plan assets in a defined contribution plan run to the employee rather than the employer. In such cases, the cost to the employer arises and should be recognized in the period in which a contribution in that amount is earned by the employees in accordance with plan provisions.

In some cases, however, a plan that has defined contribution characteristics is, in substance, a defined benefit plan. This may occur, for example, when the expected benefit levels are stated in the plan agreement and past experience indicates that the "defined" contributions are periodically adjusted to enable such stated benefits to be maintained. In such cases, the accounting we have proposed in the preceding sections of this chapter would be applicable.

To the extent that exchange transactions between an employer and an insurance company (or similarly functioning enterprise) occur where the rights and risks under the pension plan are transferred by way of an annuity contract or other means, the accounting should reflect the transfer and result in elimination of an obligation from the employer's financial statements. If, however, *all* of the risks related to the obligation for accrued benefits to date are not transferred as part of the exchange transaction, we believe that the accounting should continue to reflect the recording of a liability for the portion of the obligation not transferred.

AN OVERVIEW OF OUR PROPOSAL

If our proposal for the accounting by the employer for the costs of pension plans were to be adopted, we believe that investors and other financial statement users would benefit. Equally accepted alternatives now existing under current generally accepted accounting principles that can be applied under identical circumstances would be eliminated. The substantive liability of the employer covering the obligation for unfunded pension benefits earned to date by the employees would be recorded. The measurement of that liability would be defined in a manner that would result in elimination of alternative actuarial methods currently allowable as a basis for financial reporting (although such actuarial methods could, of course, continue to be utilized in the development of prudent funding policies). The cost of benefits attributable to the prior service of employees at the time of adoption or amendment of a pension plan would no longer implicitly (and erroneously) be deferred; and the alternative methods of amortization of such costs would therefore be eliminated. The economic resources of an enterprise and the interests of creditors and equity owners in such resources as of a specified date would be properly reflected. The changes in these interests and resources would be recorded in the period in which they actually occur.

Statements

by

Members of the Pension Research Council

concerning

A New Look at Accounting for Pension Costs

Statement by
R. A. Albright
United States Steel Corporation

We have reviewed the monograph dealing with accounting for pension costs and find that we cannot agree with what we consider to be the basic proposal outlined in the monograph that unfunded past service costs should be entered as a liability on the sponsoring company balance sheet.

Over the years we have taken the position that there is only one valid reason for improving past service benefits and that is to enhance the prospects for improved labor performance over the future by attracting and retaining competent employees. It is interesting to note that the authors of the monograph conclude that all employers have the same view as indicated in the following quote from Chapter 7:

> There is no question that employers, when they establish, revise, or negotiate with employees regarding pension plans, consider the entire cost of the plans to be an element of compensation for present and future services of their employees. Sometimes there are trade-offs between direct compensation and pension benefits. Certainly no employers today believe that they establish or supplement pension plans as rewards for past services any more than they believe that increased salaries and wages granted relate directly to past services. Decisions with respect to pension plans are forward looking.

Chapter 7 further states that "The decision to credit employees with benefits for past services may be of great value in terms of present and future employer/employee relations and in employee morale. It may even be essential to the company's continuing operations."

In view of these statements analyzing the future nature of pension plan changes, it is difficult to understand how they can arrive at the conclusion that a benefit improvement applied to both past and future service results in a cost partially applied to a prior period. We have concluded that they must have overlooked the fact that a defined benefit pension plan is a group plan under which the benefits payable in the future are earned by the group of employees working in the future. Moneys credited to the plan are not identified to individual accounts as in a defined contribution plan.

Under a defined benefit plan, all employees working in the future

85

contribute as a group to the funding of future pension benefits for the group, even though all future employees may not receive benefits. The term "past service" should not be taken literally as the authors do. It has been applied by the companies (and by the unions where the plans are negotiated) to a concept under which a fair and equitable basis was established for determining the level of pension benefits to be paid from the group plan. This no doubt was a problem faced by the first company which established a pension plan when the designers realized that, if pensions were calculated on a uniform rate and applied to future service only, someone retiring one year after the pension plan was installed would receive a very small pension, whereas those retiring after, say thirty years of participation, could receive a pension as much as thirty times greater. Under such a pension arrangement, the quality of future employee service, particularly from employees with the longest service, could hardly be expected to be stimulated.

We believe that the defined benefit pension plan group concept mandates the conclusion that increases in cost as a result of changes in pension benefit levels are truly a charge against future income, not an adjustment to prior period costs.

If, however, the authors' proposal were to be adopted, we can see potential trends that could develop to avoid having to record a fictional liability on the employer's balance sheet. The establishment of new pension plans would be discouraged since, with no advance funding, substantially all of the "past service cost" would have to be reflected as a liability on the balance sheet and such liability could appear to jeopardize the firm's financial position. Those companies which did adopt pension plans might tend strongly toward the multi-employer type of plan where the employer's liability is defined in terms of a specified contribution rate rather than in terms of defined benefits. There also could be a movement among existing defined benefit plans which have not been heavily funded to convert to multi-employer, defined contribution plans.

In another direction, there is the potential for developing a benefit rate schedule which, when applied to the future services of individual age groups, would produce essentially the same defined benefit payments as presently provided by the application of a single rate to all service. For example, the benefit schedule might provide for normal age 65 retirements, a rate with respect to future service of individuals aged 55 which would be double the rate applicable to individuals aged 45, and so forth. Such a schedule would be extremely complex, unwieldy (particularly with early retirement provisions and the back-loading provisions of ERISA), and difficult to communicate to the employees. In the end, it would accomplish nothing different insofar as benefits are concerned than the current method, and it would clearly demonstrate the group concept inherent in a defined benefit plan under which high levels of benefits are paid to persons retiring in the next few years with funds generated over the future by the group working in the future.

Any of the above actions would obviate having to record a fictional liability on the sponsor company's balance sheet.

In connection with another aspect of the authors' proposals, the valuation of plan assets at current market, we also register disagreement. They have proposed that plan assets be valued at current market. Assuming, as recommended in the foregoing, that the authors' proposal is not recognized with respect to income statements and balance sheets, the proposed method for valuing assets also should not be allowed to affect the footnotes required by the SEC with respect to unfunded liability. Pension trusts are a long-term investment medium to meet long-term pension commitments. Changes in current values of plan investments represent only unrealized gains or losses which may or may not materialize upon eventual disposition of the assets. A statement of current values as of a particular date, recognizing short-term security market fluctuations, could result in seriously over or understating values in terms of meeting long-term obligations. Such values do not provide a realistic basis for either determining the adequacy of the fund or of investment performance.

It is appropriate that a current value presentation be included with other financial information. The current value for this purpose should represent a sound underlying value of investments based on a moving average of market prices. By reporting a value which is indicative of a probable long-term realizable value rather than a realizable value at a particular date, unnecessary and inaccurate reactions of the reader would be minimized. The figure would be in keeping with the actuary's evaluations and recognize the ongoing plan concept, with which the authors concur, rather than a termination assumption which they disavow.

Statement by
Preston C. Bassett, F.S.A.
Towers, Perrin, Forster & Crosby

Accounting for pension costs is a topic of great interest to and current discussion by employers, plan sponsors, government officials, accountants and actuaries. On the other hand, it seems to be a topic of little concern to most plan participants and the public, even though the stated primary purpose of accounting for pension costs is to provide meaningful information to plan participants and the public. It just may be that we are spending too much time and energy trying to solve a difficult problem that few people really care about and for which an answer isn't needed.

The Employee Retirement Income Security Act of 1974 has forced many of us to spend hours, days, weeks and even months on relatively unimportant issues that clearly do not justify the time and effort of the individuals involved. Accounting for pension costs to meet ERISA requirements is clearly one of these. I recommend that accountants, actuaries, government officials, employers and the like adopt the forms and methods required by ERISA, interpreted in the simplest manner, and move on to more important issues. ERISA mandates that certain detailed information be given or made available to plan participants and the public. There is no justifiable need to spend more time and money preparing additional information regarding private pension plans.

But because others may disagree, I would like to comment on the monograph prepared by Mr. Hall and Mr. Landsittel. One of the primary purposes of the monograph is to develop a single recommended measure of the accrued obligation under a defined benefit pension plan.[1] The authors believe the accounting profession should require all companies to use the same method for determining their obligation at any given time for pensions earned to date, regardless of the benefit formula or how the benefits are funded (except for fully insured plans).

Their recommended method is developed in Chapter 6. They give no name to the method. Although it has been used by some actuaries, it is not a popular actuarial method since the evolving costs tend to

---

[1] Page 81.

be unstable and increase with time. Both of these characteristics generally are avoided by actuaries in their recommendations for determining the accrual of pension costs. This is acknowledged indirectly by the authors.[2] The authors have a different view of the purpose of accounting for pension costs than generally has been accepted.

APB *Opinion No. 8* went to great lengths to provide means by which sharp fluctuations in the annual charge for pension costs could be avoided—use of other than market value for assets, spreading of gains or losses, amortization of prior service costs, and so forth. The focus of APB *Opinion No. 8* was on consistency in determining the annual accrual cost of the pension plan. Pension funding was viewed as a long-term commitment that required costs to be spread out. Fluctuations and changes were to be avoided whenever possible. APB *Opinion No. 8* placed great importance on the income and outgo statement.

The authors of this monograph, however, emphasize the balance sheet and play down the importance of the income and outgo statement. The use of market values for the fund is a good illustration. Market value probably is the best measure of assets at a particular time. If market values are used at the beginning and end of the accounting period, the differences between the two values will be reflected in the income and outgo statement. Thus, pension costs will show wide variation from one accounting period to the next, depending primarily on the particular market value of the fund on the dates of measurement. The balance sheet may be "accurate," but there will be no consistency and little accuracy in the income and outgo statement.

My preference is to apply the concepts of APB *Opinion No. 8* to corporate financial statements, where, I believe, it is most important to show as expense the best estimate of the annual charge for the long-range cost of the pension plan. Market values as of a particular day are of little importance, and their use would tend to mislead the reader of the corporate financial statement.

We may arrive at a different conclusion if we examine the purpose of a financial statement of the plan itself. The purpose of the

---

[2] Page 66.

actuarial study, as explained earlier, is to develop an accrual cost for the corporation—hence, the emphasis on the income and outgo statement. However, if the purpose of the actuarial study is to advise plan participants of the security of their earned benefits, the balance sheet becomes relatively more important. How do the assets compare to the liabilities? Here we are concerned with the financial statement of the plan. The purpose is to compare the value of the fund to the liability to provide the pension and other benefits that have been promised to the participants based on their service and, perhaps, earnings to the date of valuation. Using market values for both assets and liabilities probably is the best method of measurement.

This leads me to the conclusion that it is not appropriate to use the same methods to develop the best estimate of the long-range annual cost of the pension plan for the corporation and to determine the relationship between the value of the fund and the liability to provide pension benefits for plan participants. Symmetry is quite unlikely with two different objectives. Each objective requires a separate analysis and solution. Each solution will be based on the appropriate actuarial assumptions and valuation methods to determine assets and liabilities. There is little, if any, reason for the two to be the same. To determine accrual costs for the corporate financial statement, we need a level long-range estimate of the cost to be charged to the expense statement. And to determine the accrued cost of benefits earned by plan participants, we need to measure the assets and liabilities in today's market—which may be a poor estimate for the future.

Mr. Hall and Mr. Landsittel believe that the balance sheet is paramount and that we need to compare the value of the fund to the liabilities for earned benefits. For the sake of discussion, let's accept this premise and consider the authors' recommendations.

In Chapter 6 they discuss and illustrate two actuarial methods for valuing the liabilities for earned benefits. However, they overlook a third method that is commonly used today and which, I believe, satisfies their criteria in several areas where their preferred method does not.

The first method (Tables 1 and 2) spreads costs on a level percentage of pay—5.8175% for Table 1 and 13.4672% for Table 2. The second method (Tables 3 and 4) spreads the estimated benefit at retirement in proportion to pay. The third method (not shown) accrues the benefits credited to the employee as he earns them.

Accrual of Benefits as Earned

In this last approach, the accrual of the obligation for pension benefits is directly determined by benefits earned and credited to the employee for his service to date. The obligation is the present value as of the current date of the employee's credited benefits payable at retirement.

This method is illustrated in Table 8 for a single participant whose compensation remains constant throughout the period of employment. The assumptions are the same as those in Tables 1 and 3.

Assumptions for Table 8

Hired—January 1, 1976
Retirement date—December 31, 1995
Discount rate, including an allowance both for an interest factor
    and for population decrements—12%
Present value at retirement date of estimated pension benefits:
    Base—average earnings for final three years
       prior to retirement $10,000
    Annual pension—50% of base   5,000
    Present value at retirement date, at 6%,
       assuming benefits will be paid annually
       for 12 years subsequent to the retirement
       date $5,000 × 8.38384394)   41,919

When annual compensation is assumed to remain level (Col. 2), the accrued benefit (Col. 4) increases by a constant amount—$250—each year. The accrued obligation (Col. 7) is the same as that in Table 3.

Table 9 illustrates how the Accrual of Benefits as Earned Method is applied to a more realistic situation in which compensation increases throughout the participant's employment. This table is based on the same assumptions as those made in Table 2.

Assumptions for Table 9

Hired—January 1, 1976
Retirement date—December 31, 1995
Compensation increase—8% annually compounded (includes increases assumed to result from inflation)
Discount rate, including an allowance both for an interest factor
    and for population decrements—12%

TABLE 8

Illustration of Pension Accrual Based upon Benefits earned (assuming level compensation)

(1) Year	(2) Annual Compensation	(3) Accrued Benefit Percentage*	(4) Accrued Benefit (2) × (3)	(5) Value of Accrued Benefit at Retirement†	(6) Present Value of $1 Payable at Retirement	(7) Accrued Obligation (5) × (6)
1976	$10,000	2.50%	$ 250	$ 2,096	.116106	$ 243
1977	10,000	5.00	500	4,192	.130039	545
1978	10,000	7.50	750	6,288	.145644	915
1979	10,000	10.00	1,000	8,384	.163121	1,367
1980	10,000	12.50	1,250	10,480	.182696	1,914
1981	10,000	15.00	1,500	12,576	.204619	2,573
1982	10,000	17.50	1,750	14,672	.229174	3,362
1983	10,000	20.00	2,000	16,768	.256675	4,304
1984	10,000	22.50	2,250	18,864	.287476	5,423
1985	10,000	25.00	2,500	20,960	.321973	6,749
1986	10,000	27.50	2,750	23,056	.360610	8,314
1987	10,000	30.00	3,000	25,152	.403883	10,159
1988	10,000	32.50	3,250	27,247	.452349	12,326
1989	10,000	35.00	3,500	29,343	.506631	14,867
1990	10,000	37.50	3,750	31,439	.567426	17,840
1991	10,000	40.00	4,000	33,535	.635518	21,313
1992	10,000	42.50	4,250	35,631	.711780	25,362
1993	10,000	45.00	4,500	37,727	.797193	30,076
1994	10,000	47.50	4,750	39,823	.892857	35,556
1995	10,000	50.00	5,000	41,919	1.000000	41,919

* The percentage accrued each year is 2.50% (50% ÷ 20 years).
† Col. 4 × 8.3838394 (value of an annuity payable for 12 years).

TABLE 9

Illustration of Pension Accrual Based upon Benefits Earned (assuming increasing compensation)

(1) Year	(2) Annual Compensation	(3) Accrued Benefit Percentage*	(4) 3 Year Average Compensation	(5) Accrued Benefit (3) × (4)	(6) Value of Accrued Benefit at Retirement†	(7) Present Value of $1 Payable at Retirement	(8) Accrued Obligation (6) × (7)
1976	$10,000	2.50%	$10,000	$ 250	$ 2,096	.116106	$ 243
1977	10,800	5.00	10,400	520	4,360	.130039	567
1978	11,664	7.50	10,821	812	6,808	.145644	992
1979	12,597	10.00	11,687	1,169	9,801	.163121	1,599
1980	13,605	12.50	12,622	1,578	13,230	.182696	2,417
1981	14,693	15.00	13,632	2,045	17,145	.204619	3,508
1982	15,869	17.50	14,722	2,576	21,597	.229174	4,949
1983	17,138	20.00	15,900	3,180	26,661	.256675	6,843
1984	18,509	22.50	17,172	3,864	32,395	.287476	9,313
1985	19,990	25.00	18,546	4,636	38,867	.321973	12,514
1986	21,589	27.50	20,029	5,508	46,178	.360610	16,652
1987	23,316	30.00	21,632	6,489	54,403	.403883	21,972
1988	25,182	32.50	23,362	7,593	63,658	.452349	28,796
1989	27,196	35.00	25,231	8,831	74,038	.506631	37,510
1990	29,372	37.50	27,250	10,219	85,674	.567426	48,614
1991	31,722	40.00	29,430	11,772	98,695	.635518	62,722
1992	34,259	42.50	31,784	13,508	113,249	.711780	80,608
1993	37,000	45.00	34,327	15,447	129,505	.797193	103,240
1994	39,960	47.50	37,073	17,610	147,639	.892857	131,821
1995	43,157	50.00	40,039	20,020	167,845	1.000000	167,845

* The percentage accrued each year is 2.50% (50% ÷ 20 years).
† Col. 5 × 8.38384394 (value of an annuity payable for 12 years).

Present value at retirement date of estimated pension benefits:
Base—average earnings for final three years
prior to retirement $40,039
Annual pension—50% of base 20,020
Present value at retirement date, at 6%,
assuming benefits will be paid annually for
12 years subsequent to the retirement date
($20,020 × 8.38384394) 167,845

The Accrual of Benefits as Earned Method measures the obligation of the employer at any time for the benefits that have been credited to the employee. For example, if the employee quits with a vested benefit in 1990, his accrued annual benefit payable at retirement would be $10,219 (Col. 5). This is true regardless of the method used to compute the accrued obligation. This benefit is determined by the provisions of the plan (full vesting after ten years of service, for example). The value of this benefit in 1990 is $48,614. However, only the third method produces this value. The first method, Table 2, produces a value of $77,482 and the second method, Table 4, a value of $56,508. Only the third method, Accrual of Benefits as Earned, measures the obligation for benefits earned to date.

The distinction between the methods recommended by the authors and this method is that the former includes in the benefits accrued to date the effect of inflation and salary increases that may be granted to the employee in future years up to retirement. In other words, the accrued benefit includes future and unknown pay increases. Some would consider this inconsistent with the criterion that the obligation should measure only the value of benefits earned to date—not benefits that may be credited in the future if and when the employee receives pay increases. There appears to be little justification to include in the obligation of the plan sponsor the cost of future pay increases.

The following statements by the authors would seem to support this position:

1. They "would exclude from the balance sheet of a business enterprise deferred charges and other intangible assets. . . ."[3] If this holds true for liabilities as well, which would be a logical assumption, future uncertain pay increases should be excluded as well.

---
[3] Pages 23–24.

2. ". . . the statements should not attempt to present a projection or prediction of . . . unearned obligations."[4]

In summary, I have difficulty in accepting the authors' recommended method, their second method, for determining the obligation for pension benefits to be shown on the balance sheet. For this purpose, the Accrual of Benefits as Earned Method appears to provide a more accurate measure of the current obligation.

However, I believe, as stated earlier, that the primary emphasis should be on the corporate income and outgo statement. Therefore, if I must choose one method for all purposes from among these three methods, I would select the first since it:

1. Produces a stable cost, at least in theory.
2. Is easily understood by the layman, being similar to the cost of the purchase of an endowment life insurance policy.
3. Is not conservative, as the authors imply, because it accumulates only the funds estimated to be necessary to provide the benefits promised under the plan.
4. Assumes that the plan will continue in effect and not terminate.
5. May be used for both the corporate financial statement and the plan financial statement.
6. Is suitable for all current purposes of pension plan cost determinations.
7. Is a widely used and acceptable method in the pension world.

Now back to my original question: Is all this discussion and concern about accounting for pension costs necessary or desirable? Probably not. After all, ERISA is sufficient to assure that plan participants and the public can obtain all the information they need, and more. Plan sponsors and financial analysts also have access to additional information. Furthermore, *APB Opinion No. 8* has worked well for ten years. ERISA has produced—and continues to produce— major problems for plan sponsors, and the climate is not favorable to introduce more complications of questionable value.

My recommendation: Do not add further complications or require additional cost calculations. Make only those changes that are absolutely necessary for all parties concerned. In short, work toward making compliance with ERISA as simple as possible.

---

[4] Page 42.

Statement by
Edwin F. Boynton, F.S.A.
The Wyatt Company

The "new look" at accounting for pension costs indeed presents a different approach to the subject in many respects. Unfortunately, a new look does not necessarily produce a "better answer." Over the years the pages of actuarial literature have presented a fairly broad range of technically sound funding methods which develop actuarial liability figures useful for various purposes. Admittedly, despite the technical soundness of these various definitions of "accrued actuarial liability," the multiplicity of methods has led to confusion on the part of the "public," including not only the accounting profession but attorneys, financial executives, and government legislators and regulators.

While the actuarial profession would be well-advised to clarify the purposes of various definitions of "accrued actuarial liability," and indeed is in the process of doing so, clearly what is *not* needed at the present time is a new definition, established for accounting purposes, which lacks any sound actuarial foundation. Perhaps even more significant and controversial is that the quantity so defined would, under the authors' proposal, become a liability on the plan sponsor's balance sheet, without regard to the actual legal liabilities inherent in the plan documents or imposed by applicable Federal statutes.

It is of interest to note that in a work which is designated as a research project, the authors have failed to make any analysis of the existing actuarial methods which produce an accrued liability, or to indicate where such methods might be inconsistent with the theory underlying generally accepted accounting principles. It would seem logical that before promoting the development of a new, nonactuarial method of defining the accrued liability, the authors would discuss why existing actuarial methods are not sufficient for their purposes.

The authors have basically defined an "accrued obligation" for their purposes by taking a percentage of the present value of future benefits; such percentage is developed essentially by taking the ratio of (*a*) accumulated compensation for service to date as an employee to (*b*) projected compensation at retirement, such values being adjusted for interest during the respective periods. While this is an interesting approach, it has very little theoretical support to justify it, except, perhaps as an alternative to the approach used in certain types of plans (e.g., offset plans), which define an accrued benefit by applying a ratio based on service to date to projected service at retirement.

One of the concepts expressed by the authors is that the "obligation for plan benefits should be recorded in pension plan financial statements as such benefits are *earned* by the employees," a statement that seems very reasonable. However, their particular interpretation of "earned" is that every benefit is earned in a proportion related to accumulated compensation, regardless of the type of plan. There seems to be no justification offered as to why "the most appropriate method of measuring that portion of the benefits that has been earned to date is to correlate the recording of the obligation with employee compensation costs." The authors apparently just intuitively feel that it should be done in this way.

Many observers would agree with the concept of recording obligations for plan benefits as such benefits are earned, as stated by the authors. However, since each is supposed to provide a clear and concise definition of how benefits are earned, this would seem to be a far more logical foundation for establishing a liability for earned benefits. Many examples are available of plan formulas where the determination of the "accrued obligation" in the suggested fashion (by relating it to total accumulated compensation) makes little sense, such as a future-service-only plan, a plan where the past service benefits are determined in significantly different fashion from future service benefits, flat dollar type benefits which are unrelated to compensation, and so forth. A fundamental flaw in the suggested approach is that it ignores the plan provisions altogether, which, if properly drafted, define precisely how benefits are "earned" under the plan. But nothing is offered in support of the accrued compensation argument except the authors' belief that that is the way it should be.

More practically, to anyone familiar with the nature of employee records held by many plan sponsors, the determination of the obligation in this suggested fashion would present monumental problems and expense. When one realizes that many large employers have difficulty even knowing the number of employees on the payroll at a given point in time, the problems of gathering and organizing the data required by this method are mind-boggling.

The developments leading up to ERISA and the law itself have underscored the importance of communicating plan provisions as clearly as possible to plan participants and the public in general.

This suggested approach would seem to add one more dimension to the existing level of complications. ERISA places upon the actuary the responsibility for the determination of the actuarial liabilities of the plan based on his judgment as to future anticipated experience and accepted funding methods. Such information is either given to or available to plan participants in the actuarial statement as a part of Form 5500. To suggest that the obligation for accrued plan benefits be determined in a manner completely inconsistent with the plan provisions and with the actuarial liabilities determined by the enrolled actuary throws up one more barrier to adequate communication to participants. The plan participants who review annual reports filed with the Labor Department would certainly be confused by one set of actuarial liability figures appearing in the actuarial statement prepared by the enrolled actuary, and a completely different set of liabilities appearing in a GAAP accounting statement prepared by the qualified accountant.

It is also of interest to note that the Committee Report accompanying the ERISA legislation strongly urged that consistent actuarial standards be used for all plan purposes, including not only financial statements of the plan itself but the financial reports for the employer.

The other major controversial idea injected by the authors is the concept that the accrued liabilities of the pension plan, however defined, should be shown as liabilities of the company on the balance sheet. The practical difficulties of doing this immediately have led the authors to propose a modification of the basic concept as a transitional arrangement. Otherwise a great many companies might be thrown into technical or actual bankruptcy by being required to include liabilities in their balance sheet which are not legal liabilities at all.

The proposal to present unfunded accrued liabilities of the pension plan on a company balance sheet has long been discussed, but as pointed out in the historical development presented by the authors, the concept was rejected by the accounting profession many years ago. Philosophical discussions as to the nature of the pension plan obligations went on for many years, but ERISA seems to have clearly established the definition of the ultimate potential employer liability. From a layman's viewpoint, ERISA provides that the potential liability of an employer is for the unfunded value of vested benefits, up to a maximum of 30 percent of the employer's net worth (unless mitigated by contingent. employer liability insurance which might be offered at some future date). Most informed persons (including accountants) seem to believe that even this should not be shown as a liability on the balance sheet of a company, unless the probability of termination of a plan is reasonably high. Certainly it is an item of interest as a footnote to the balance sheet, but it would not seem appropriate to put it on the balance sheet of a company whose probability of termination of the plan is very low, in the same way that liability suits against a company which seem to be without merit are disregarded on the balance sheet.

In any event, even if it should be decreed (by SEC, FASB, etc.) that certain pension plan liabilities be shown on the company balance sheet, it would seem that ERISA has defined the amount of potential legal liability, which is the value of vested benefits, and not an artificial value of all accrued benefits.

Finally, from a practical viewpoint, the adoption of this approach would be a major hindrance to the adoption of new plans or significant amendment of existing plans. This consideration should certainly not be controlling if there is some logical reason why such a liability should be shown on the balance sheet. However, the arguments presented by the authors are not sufficient to put such a stumbling block in the road of the sound development of pension plans providing adequate past service benefits. The value to the company and the public of providing for sound and adequate retirement plans is too important to be undermined by the theoretical accounting arguments presented by the authors.

It is always awkward to write critically in public print of a well-prepared statement prepared by two obviously experienced practitioners in the accounting field; it is unfortunate that such a well-written and well-constructed presentation arrives at recommendations which appear to me to be basically unsound and unwise.

Statement by
Laurence E. Coward
William M. Mercer Limited

Although I admire the approach of the authors to accounting for pension costs, I must dissent from the proposed requirements that pension fund assets should always be valued at market price.

Actuarial valuations involve placing a value on both assets and liabilities of the pension plan. It is, I think, universally agreed that the two sides to the balance sheet are not independent but should be valued by consistent methods and assumptions. The authors are obviously comfortable with the assets side, but apparently less so with the liabilities side which essentially they would leave to actuarial judgment. It seems, therefore, that the authors have taken the problems and thrown them over to the actuary's side of the fence. They would value assets at market which implies a certain view of the social, political and economic future; they would then have 'the actuary value the pension benefits from the same viewpoint.

In Chapter 3 it states "In the preparation of financial statements, there should be an appropriate balance between subjectivity, which contributes to relevance, and objectivity, which increases verifiability. Practice today is weighted far too heavily on the side of objectivity—almost to the extent of making objectivity an end rather than a means." Is this comment not applicable to the proposed method of asset valuation? Market value is the best or only asset valuation method if a fund is to be terminated, but is not necessarily the best if the fund is to continue in effect for many years.

More important, the valuation of assets and liabilities must be on a consistent basis. If current market is the only proper way to value the investments, should not current market equally be used to value the liabilities? In this case, the liabilities would be determined by a competitive insurance company's quotations for deferred annuities and other benefits earned to date under terms of the plan.

Under ERISA the valuation of assets must "reflect" changes in market value but the use of market value is not required. Smoothed equity values and amortized bond values are permitted. An actuary who, in accordance with the guidelines of his profession, has prepared a valuation that satisfies the Internal Revenue Service and ERISA and his client, should not have to do another valuation for accounting purposes.

The dilemma might be solved if the accounting profession were willing to show assets at market value and to allow the inclusion of a further item which might be called "Actuary's Investment Reserve." It must be admitted that this item does not meet the criteria laid down by the authors for inclusion in financial statements.

Accountants would be quite right to reject a situation where another profession specifies the income side of a revenue account and asks the accountant to prepare the outgo side and to certify the results. It is no more proper that actuaries should be asked to do much the same thing in their professional field.

From a practical standpoint if market value were used for assets, the valuation rate of interest would have to change at each valuation. It would usually be a fractional amount. The market value of investments and the value of pension liabilities are both sensitive to interest rate changes—since both involve present values of future cash flows. Hence if asset values fall, presumably the actuary's valuation interest rate should rise, which means that to achieve realistic results the actuary might have to value at 6.22 percent in one year, 5.17 percent the next, 8.30 percent the third, and so forth. There would be no continuity in the valuation results and much valuable information as to the progress of this fund would be lost. (This information could be obtained by double or treble valuations but only with considerable trouble and expense.)

I believe that the financial statements for a pension fund should allow assets to be valued at other than market value, provided the valuation meets the other criteria laid down by the authors. The company's financial statements should show the unfunded liability or surplus as certified by the actuary in the actuarial valuation of the pension fund.

One thing is clear—the accounting and actuarial professions should get together to make sure each has full understanding of and confidence in the work of the other.

Statement by
John K. Dyer, Jr., F.S.A.
Independent Actuary

An actuary has been defined as a person who "proceeds in a mathematically straight line from an erroneous assumption to a foregone conclusion." Despite its excellent organization and lucid development, the Hall-Landsittel manuscript causes me to wonder if this definition is not equally applicable to accountants.

There a number of assumptions postulated by Hall and Landsittel which, while hardly "erroneous" are in fact contrary to long standing and widely accepted practice both by actuaries and accountants. Perhaps the key to most of these is the concept of "smoothing" as applied to financial reporting—a concept which the authors reject as inappropriate for pension accounting. The most conspicuous results of this approach are their conclusions that current market value should be the basis for valuation of pension fund assets, and that actuarial gains and losses should be recognized in full as they appear.

I would first question whether the rejection of "smoothing" is in any way consistent with the universal accounting practices of depreciating physical property over an assumed useful lifetime, and depleting natural resources over an assumed period of recovery. It seems to me that these procedures are no more nor less than "smoothing" devices.

Turning to a more purely financial framework, the life insurance business almost universally amortizes premiums and accrues discounts in valuing bonds purchased at prices different from their maturity values, in some cases producing results quite different from their current market values. Here again we see a widely used "smoothing" device that insurance accountants and regulatory authorities have long accepted as standard.

Even within the context of pension accounting, the authors have failed to carry their repudiation of "smoothing" to its logical conclusion. Would it not be more consistent with their concept to recognize that a pension benefit "accrual" does not become a real liability until it is vested, that is, until the point in time when it becomes a contractual obligation? Up to that point it is contingent upon the employee's survival and continuing service, and even after the vesting requirements are met the allocation of any part of the accrued benefit to the pre-vesting period is essentially a "smoothing" process.

A more noticeable inconsistency lies in the authors' insistence upon valuing assets at current market, while accepting the valuation of liabilities on the basis of classical actuarial "present value" methods. To resolve this inconsistency would require either: (a) Valuation of the liabilities at "market" by applying to accrued benefits the premiums required to purchase and guarantee them in a competitive insurance market, or (b) Valuation of the assets on a "present value" basis, whereby both cost and market values are ignored and each security is valued by discounting, at the same interest rate used to value the liabilities, the expected future income and return of capital.

The "present value" basis for valuing assets is widely used in the United Kingdom, and to some extent in Canada and Europe, but has not been used to any extent in the United States.

Perhaps the real source of these difficulties and anomolies is that the authors have embraced two concepts that are essentially incompatible—the "presumption that the enterprise will continue to exist and function," and the rejection of spreading of costs and smoothing of income. Is it not inherent in a "going concern" balance sheet that some elements of smoothing are always present, and that the elimination of all such elements results in what is, almost by definition, a "liquidation" balance sheet?

Notwithstanding what seem to be fundamental flaws in their reasoning, the authors have produced a readable and provocative study. While it seems unlikely that their conclusions will be accepted by pension actuaries, they have most assuredly fulfilled their assignment as described by Dr. McGill "to set forth a coherent, theoretical framework within which the (pension accounting) issues could be considered and hopefully resolved in a rational way." The number and variety of dissents being submitted, even before publication, are clear evidence that the study is already serving its purpose in provoking thoughtful reexamination of this important but too much neglected aspect of private pensions.

Statement by
Donald S. Grubbs, Jr.
George B. Buck Consulting Actuaries, Inc.

Through this monograph Messrs. Hall and Landsittel will serve a most valuable function of causing readers to make a fresh examination of the bases of pension plan accounting. However, there are important reasons why a number of their conclusions should be rejected.

The monograph states that financial statements of plans and of employers must be adapted to the needs of users. A brief survey of the principal users of each and their needs may thus be helpful.

The Needs of Users of Financial Statements of the Plan

Prior to ERISA an extremely small proportion of pension plans themselves had a financial statement prepared by an independent accountant. For the majority of plans the statements of assets and of the changes in assets were generally prepared by the bank or insurance company funding the plan. The principal exceptions were for those plans not wholly funded by a bank or insurance company, and for some multiemployer plans regardless of the funding medium. If those responsible for plans had felt that the statements prepared by banks and insurance companies were inadequate, they could have engaged an independent accountant to prepare a separate financial statement, but they generally felt no such need.

Under ERISA the plan administrator must file with both the Department of Labor and the Internal Revenue Service an annual report for the plan using Form 5500, Form 5500–C or Form 5500–K. The report includes a statement of assets and liabilities and a statement of income, expenses and changes in net assets, which must be completed in accordance with the form and its instructions regardless of whether this agrees with generally accepted accounting principles. If he desires, the plan administrator can seek assistance of an accountant, actuary or other person. For most defined benefit plans the plan administrator must attach Schedule B, prepared by the actuary, containing information on compliance with the minimum funding requirements. For plans with 100 or more participants (less than 5 percent of all plans but covering over 50 percent of all plan participants) a statement of an independent accountant must be attached to the copy of Form 5500 to be filed with the Department of Labor. For all plans a summary of the annual report must be provided to plan participants.

For those plans for which an accountant's statement is prepared, the potential users include participants, employers, fiduciaries, actuaries and governmental agencies. The needs of these users vary. The participants theoretically have an interest in what benefits the plan would be able to provide if it were terminated and in what benefits it will be able to provide if continued; in practice they almost never are concerned about these questions in an ongoing plan, and most would have difficulty understanding a financial statement. Fiduciaries may need financial information to determine that ERISA fiduciary requirements are met. Employers may want financial information for the plan to evaluate the asset management or to complete the employer's own financial statements. The actuary needs financial information to determine the asset value for actuarial purposes, to determine the date and amount of contributions, and to select appropriate actuarial assumptions. The Department of Labor may need financial information for enforcement of fiduciary requirements. The various users may obtain this information from financial statements or information provided by the accountant, bank, insurance company, actuary, employer and/or plan administrator. To the extent the needs are not met by other sources, the users will look to the financial statements for the plan, as certified by the accountant.

The IRS also requires financial information to enforce the funding requirements and to review deduction of contributions and possible prohibited transactions. Significantly, IRS reached the conclusion that the forms, *without the accountant's report*, will provide the information it needs.

Another need is to keep the administrative costs of the plan low. All expenses either increase the cost of the plan to employers or reduce the benefits which can be provided to employees. Unnecessary expense for duplicating accounting, actuarial or administrative services should be avoided.

Needs of Users of Financial Statements of the Employer

The principal users of the financial statements of the employer are management, investors and creditors, together with financial analysts who may serve them. Management will normally obtain any necessary information from reports prepared for the plan by the actuary, bank and/or insurance company. These users may be interested in knowing the plan's effect on the employer's net worth and on its past and future earnings. They may be interested in a best estimate view, a conservative view or both. Municipalities, states and the federal government have different users of their financial statements, with different needs.

Symmetry

The users of the plan's financial statements have needs quite different from those of users of the employer's statements. The artistic value of symmetry should not stand in the way of meeting the needs of users.

The Impact of ERISA

The monograph makes a number of references to the effect of ERISA on accounting requirements, without exploring the specific requirements of ERISA and the effect of the specific requirements.

ERISA's requirements as to who must receive financial reports were discussed above.

Both before and after ERISA, the employer was required ultimately to fund the benefits defined in the plan if the plan was not discontinued. The minimum funding requirements of ERISA do establish minimum requirements on the timing of contributions. If the minimum funding requirements are not satisfied, the funding deficiency plus an excise tax are legal liabilities of the employer which should be shown on the employer's balance sheet. The monograph ignores this legal liability on the employer's balance sheet. It does not relate the employer's provision for pension cost to the ERISA minimum funding requirements, although those minimums place a floor on the employer's actual contributions. Thus the monograph is inconsistently maintaining that ERISA has affected the employer's cost and liability for an ongoing plan, while simultaneously ignoring its actual changes.

The monograph also indicates that ERISA's provisions relating to terminating plans affect the employer's financial statements, while ignoring the specific effects of those provisions. On plan termination the employer's liability under Section 4062 of ERISA equals the excess of the current value of the plan's guaranteed benefits over the plan's assets applicable to such benefits, or 30 percent of the employer's net worth, if less. However, if the employer has contingent liability coverage under Section 4023 of ERISA, the employer's liability is $0, completely insulating the employer from all pension obligations other than the minimum funding requirements of ERISA. PBGC is considering requiring all employers to have contingent liability coverage. But the monograph is not arguing that ERISA liability be shown on the balance sheet. I do not maintain that the termination provisions of ERISA should, for a continuing plan, affect the employer's financial statements. But, after correctly ignoring these specific plan termination provisions, the monograph somehow argues that they still affect the employer's liability.

The monograph also ignores the potential termination liability which may accrue to an employer participating in a multiemployer or multiple-employer plan.

Employer Balance Sheet

The monograph calls for recognition of "substantive" liabilities. The liabilities which really have substance at year end are the amounts known to be actually paid after year end plus any legal liabilities for payments. In addition to these substantive amounts it may be appropriate to record a liability for any other amounts accrued but unpaid at year end. Thus for an ongoing plan the appropriate employer liability should be (a) any accrued but unpaid contributions as of the end of the fiscal period (as under *Opinion* 8) plus (b) any funding deficiency not included in such accrual.

On the other hand, for a plan expected to be terminated in the near future the appropriate liability is any payment to PBGC required by ERISA Section 4062 which is not relieved by the contingent liability insurance of Section 4023.

The unfunded liability of the plan is not a liability of the employer. The authors acknowledge that past service benefits are often established in consideration of future employment, and that the employer has no legal liability for their payment. As previously indicated, ERISA gives no basis for the employer including any liability other than a funding deficiency or, in the case of a terminating plan, any payment due PBGC under Section 4062.

The monograph presents an analogy between a pension plan's unfunded liability and research and development costs. The FASB concluded that research and development costs should be charged to expense as incurred and should not be capitalized as deferred charges and amortized in future periods, even though such costs would benefit future periods. However, research and development costs are generally costs already paid or payable, which cannot be escaped no matter what happens in the future. Unfunded pension liabilities, on the other hand, need not be paid currently and may be avoided entirely if the plan is terminated (as 4,500 pension plans were in 1975) for any one of many reasons.

If the objective of financial statements is to provide investors or creditors with a picture of substantive liabilities, it is the legal liabilities of ERISA which have substance, not an actuarial reflection of costs to be paid over many years in the future for plans established in consideration of future employment. This is particularly apparent if, as the authors recommend, the accrued liability is calculated based on a projection of future salaries rather than current salaries.

Even if the difference between assets and accrued liabilities were to be included on the employer's balance sheet, it would be improper to require use of current market value for this purpose. The authors state that the accrued liabilities should be determined on the assumption of an ongoing plan, and I submit that this concept is also essential to the valuation of assets. Pension plan investments are generally long-term investments. Common stocks are usually purchased to achieve long-term growth and such growth, not the day-to-day fluctuations of the market, is the important consideration. An appropriate measure of asset values recognizes such long-term growth through devices such as average market value over five years. In the case of high grade bonds expected to be held to maturity, current market value is an inappropriate value. Furthermore, the actuarial investment return assumption is related to the actuarial valuation of assets, both determined on a going-concern basis.

The monograph focuses most of its attention on situations where the plan's liabilities exceed its assets, but also mentions that any excess of the plan's assets over its accrued liabilities should be included as an asset on the employer's balance sheet. Many plans have been funded under a projected level cost method that determines costs as a level percentage of payroll, or level dollars per covered employee, producing substantially larger accrued liabilities than the method prescribed by the authors. Many of these plans are fully funded or almost fully funded on this basis, and the authors' proposal would result in substantial assets appearing on the employer's balance sheet. These "excess" assets resulted largely from prior year contributions determined in prior years. It is doubtful that creditors and investors would regard such "excess" assets in the plan's irrevocable trust fund as assets of the employer, or that this proposal would provide the meaningful information sought by knowledgeable users.

The monograph indicates that, in calculating the plan's accrued liability, benefits should be assumed to accrue at a uniform percentage of compensation, past and future. The authors present two methods of developing the accrued liability and recommend the so-called "benefit correlated method". The method is actually a modification of the accrued benefit cost method with projection, and with a substitution of earnings for years of service as the basis for allocation of costs. The accrued liability developed under this method is lower than that generated by any actuarial cost method in general use.

On the other hand the "cost correlated method," which is considered and rejected, is a modification of the entry age normal cost method with the normal cost computed as a level percentage of payroll. This method is widely used and generates an accrued liability higher than all other actuarial cost methods.

Moreover, a substantial portion of pension plan liabilities in the United States is represented by plans where benefits are unrelated to compensation, including most collectively bargained plans. Under such plans it would seem more appropriate to allocate costs or benefits uniformly as a flat dollar amount over the employee's working lifetime without relation to compensation.

The monograph indicates a different treatment for those insured plans where the "rights and risks under the plan are transferred" to the insurance company. To the extent of such transfer, the employer's balance sheet would not need to reflect the difference between the assets and accrued liabilities. Plans fully funded with level premium individual or group contracts would require no entry on the employer's balance sheet. Thus if two identical companies had identical pension plans, except that one funded its plan with a trust or deposit administration contract and the other funded its plan with group level premium annuities, and if they made identical contributions, the two companies would have very different results in their balance sheet and in the profit and loss statement. Yet each of the two companies will need to make approximately the same outlay for pensions in future years if the plans are continued. In either case future experience differing from that expected will increase or decrease the employer's outlay, either directly or through the experience rating process. It is doubtful that this would accomplish the goals of gaining acceptance from businessmen, accountants and knowledgeable users or of conveying meaningful information to them.

One of the more complex concepts, ignored by the monograph, is the problem of comparing levels of pension benefits for different plan sponsors. Pension benefits related to average final compensation may hold up for many years. On the other hand, benefits related to career compensation or benefit amounts unrelated to compensation are usually expected to be amended at more frequent intervals. The legal barriers which prevent the measurement of liabilities under such plans on a basis comparable to prevalent accepted practice applicable to average final compensation plans appear insuperable. Failure to meet and answer this problem constitutes, perhaps, the single most glaring defect in any measurement of the pension obligation.

The monograph proposes that either the plan's balance sheet or a footnote should show the plan's value of vested benefits. *APB Opinion No. 8* requires the disclosure of the *unfunded* value of vested benefits (which is what really matters), not the value of vested benefits themselves. Frequently the actuary can be 100 percent certain that the unfunded value of vested benefits is $0 without actually calculating the value of vested benefits, as when the assets exceed the calculated value of all accrued benefits. In these circumstances calculation of the value of vested benefits adds unnecessary work and expense on the part of the actuary, particularly in plans with graded vesting. Since financial statements are adapted to needs, unnecessary calculations should be avoided. Full disclosure of the basis of the calculations is, however, most desirable, including a statement of the value of assets used for the comparison.

Employer Profit and Loss Statement

The monograph's proposal to show as a charge (or credit!) for pension expense the increase or decrease in its proposed balance sheet entries would result in entries which fluctuate wildly from year to year and which would give readers of the financial statement no guidance as to what to expect in the future. It would lead some employers to make poor policy decisions in order to avoid showing apparent losses in the financial statement. For example, a pension fund invested entirely in short-term Treasury bills could provide much more stability to the financial statement than one invested in common stocks or long-term bonds. This might mislead statement readers into thinking that the employer investing its pension fund in stocks and bonds had performed poorly in a year when market values declined, even though it was following a policy generally recognized as more prudent than investing entirely in short-term bills.

A change in actuarial assumptions is often made in a year in which it has no relation to any events which have occurred. But under the proposed method this could have an extreme effect upon the profit and loss statement. This would not only make financial statements misleading through inadvertence, but could invite manipulation and bring undesirable pressures on the actuary in the area of changes in assumptions.

The authors criticize the variety of the patterns of cost recognition in use, which results from differing actuarial methods and assumptions and from differing amortization periods. Actuarial assumptions must be considered, in the aggregate and in combination with the actuarial cost method, as potential trend lines applied to estimate emerging pension expense. In this regard the actuarial valuation of assets forms a similar function.

It is entirely appropriate to use differing patterns of cost recognition for plans where benefits are related to pay rather than those which have benefits unrelated to pay, for plans with past service benefits as opposed to plans with no past service benefits, for plans with benefits related to each year's current pay as distinguished from plans with benefits related to final average pay, for companies with differing workforces, for companies with differing economic forecasts, and so forth. Precise uniformity does not, in fact, exist and would mask the very real differences in plans.

Additional Topics Needing Consideration

It would be impossible for such a monograph to cover every aspect of pension plan accounting. Any consideration of the adoption of the authors' proposals should include exploration of the corporate obligation under the following additional topics:

1. Collectively bargained multiemployer plans.
2. Multiple-employer plans.

3. Other collectively bargained plans under which the employer's contributions are defined in the collective bargaining agreement and the benefits of participants are defined in the plan.
4. Modification of the definition of accrued benefit for accounting purposes when the plan provides a different rate of benefit accrual for past service than for future service, or when a plan provides benefits for future service only.
5. Target benefit plans.
6. The transition from present accounting practices to the proposed practices.
7. The impact on financial statements of municipal, state and federal governmental units.

Effect of Proposals

Adoption of the authors' proposals would affect various employers and various plans in many differing ways. Some of these are the following:

1. Some corporations which are actually in very sound financial condition would be shown to have a negative net worth; other corporations in less favorable financial condition could have their net worth substantially increased.
2. The profit and loss statement would show great fluctuations from year to year due to actuarial gains and losses (including investment market volatility), changes in actuarial assumptions and plan amendments.
3. Some employers would change to funding their plans through level premium annuities to escape the above effects, even though they might be adversely affected by higher actual future costs.
4. Some trustees would shift to investments with little fluctuation in market values, such as short-term Treasury bills, without regard to the best interests of either plan participants or plan sponsors.
5. Some employers would shift from final pay plans to career average pay plans with occasional updating of past service providing approximately the same benefits with substantially reduced accrued liability.
6. Some employers would shift from a defined benefit pension plan to the combination of (a) a defined contribution plan and (b) a defined benefit plan under which the benefit is offset by that

provided under the defined contribution plan, providing the same benefits as before but with substantially reduced accrued liability.

7. Some employers would change to target benefit plans, providing approximately the same benefits with no accrued liability.

8. Financial statements would be distorted by the above.

In summary, utmost care must be given to any prescribed measurement of the pension obligation in the corporate financial statements. As indicated above, the consequences could be equally detrimental to the best interests of plan participants and the future financial obligations of the plan sponsor.

It is, in my opinion, quite erroneous to conclude that a smaller unfunded accrued liability, or unfunded vested liability, represents a stronger long-range financial position for either the plan or the plan sponsor. The lower figure may well represent (a) an unrecognized potential liability under a multiemployer or a multiple-employer plan or (b) a deferral of plan amendments; while the higher figure may well represent a fictitious amount in a plan termination situation.

Statement by
E. L. Hicks
Arthur Young & Company

William Hall and David Landsittel have presented a provocative and interesting analysis of their views about accounting for pension cost. Their investigation is timely. For one thing, it has been just about ten years since the APB issued its *Opinion No. 8*, "Accounting for the Cost of Pension Plans." That Opinion, when issued, was widely recognized as an interim, compromise step toward improved accounting.[1] For another thing, the enactment of ERISA has drawn attention to various aspects of pension plans, including the principles for recognizing their cost. These two considerations, among others, have led the FASB to put the question of accounting for pension cost on its formal agenda.

For several reasons, it would not serve a useful purpose to comment extensively in this note on the conclusions presented in the monograph. The authors have acknowledged in the Preface that readers will not necessarily agree with their views; the members of the Pension Research Council, in authorizing publication of a research monograph, do not necessarily endorse the conclusions expressed; and the remarks of several of the other members of the Council, included along with this note, support points of view other than those advanced in the monograph. Nevertheless, it may be in order to call attention to one or two matters.

A central question is whether prior service cost—the present value of the element of an employer's ultimate future outlay for pensions that will arise because benefits are to be based in part on employees' service prior to the date of the employer's financial statements being prepared—should give rise to a liability in the employer's balance sheet. This is a complicated issue, involving simultaneously a perception of the nature of past-service cost and a perception of the nature, for accounting purposes, of a liability. The authors have found that past-service cost, to the extent not funded,

---

[1] Paragraph 17 of *APB Opinion No. 8* included the following: "The Board has concluded, in the light of . . . [existing] differences in views and of the fact that accounting for pension costs is in a transitional stage, that the range of practices would be significantly narrowed if pension costs were accounted for at the present time within limits . . . [described in the Opinion]." (Emphasis supplied.)

ought to be presented as a liability. Given their perceptions of past-service cost and liabilities, it is easy enough to follow their path to that conclusion. But their perceptions of both matters are controversial.

The authors have based some of their conclusions on certain general objectives they believe should be adopted for financial statements. In this aspect of the monograph, the authors have prejudged and oversimplified some of the most important and difficult matters facing accountants, matters that have high priority on the FASB's agenda in its project to establish a conceptual framework for accounting and reporting. The issues in that project are so intricate that it is not practicable to comment usefully, in this necessarily brief note, on the authors' choice of proposed objectives. Let it suffice to point out, first, that differing objectives may ultimately be selected and, second, that other accountants might reach different conclusions in applying the authors' generalized formulation of objectives to a specific question of accounting principle.

Statement by
Robert Tilove
Martin E. Segal Company

Since pension costs have become substantial in relation to profits, it is understandable that accountants have become more interested in the proper accounting of pension costs. Messrs. Hall and Landsittel show commendable independence in providing their own concept of accounting standards.

However, it is not, in my opinion, the right answer. Their analysis would have benefitted from more extensive consideration of actuarial concepts and practices.

The central part of their prescription is that a company's earnings should reflect in full any change in the unfunded present value of accrued benefits.[1] A liberalization of the plan or the effect of a change in actuarial assumptions would be reflected—in full—in the year when the amendment or the change in valuation was effective.

It is difficult to visualize that sort of accounting as meeting the ultimate test of usefulness to the user of the financial report. Any user would immediately want to know how to translate a charge so abrupt and nonrepetitive into a charge spread over a relevant period of years.

Messrs. Hall and Landsittel reject smoothing or spreading on the ground that a "liability" ought to be recognized in full when it exists. It is difficult to understand, however, why the unfounded accrued benefits must be regarded as a liability. They recognize that it is not a legal liability, either of the plan or of the company. Yet they offer no reason to regard it as a liability, giving nothing more than an essentially circular reiteration that it is.

What they fail to recognize is that the concept of "benefit accrual" with each year of an employee's service is nothing more or less than the smoothing of an ultimate pension obligation.

Perhaps they have been misled by the fact that pension terminology refers to "benefit accrual" and to "past service liability" even when no legal obligation has been incurred.

Suppose a pension plan vests benefits of $100 a month after 10 years of service. Before an employee has completed 10 years of

---

[1] We disregard, for the sake of simplicity, the special basis proposed for prorating projected benefits to each of the years of service.

service, an obligation to pay has not been "accrued." Yet we use the word "accrued" in reference to the value of $10 of monthly benefits for each year of service. This involves two different meanings of "accrued"—the first refers to the incurring of a legal obligation; the second refers to a logical *prorating* to each of the component years of the obligation that may ultimately be incurred. The proration is nothing more or less than a smoothing process.

Apparently, without realizing it, the authors treat the sum of amounts allocated for the purpose of smoothing as if they were financial liabilities.

A smoothing procedure is necessary, but one particular method cannot be singled out as inevitable on the ground that it is not smoothing at all.

The proposed standard would introduce into company financial statements a confusion from which users would have to be rescued through further explanations by accountants and financial analysts.

With respect to public employee retirement systems, the proposed standards would wreak havoc. They would require state and local governments (and the federal government?) to carry the unfunded present value of accrued benefits as if it were part of government debt. That would be a bold step in precisely the wrong direction. Certainly, governments should recognize unflinchingly the full costs of their retirement systems. However, the Draconian solution of requiring them to treat the unfunded value as debt begs the question as to what is appropriate as funding policy for a public body. The authors do not really discuss this question at all, making no more than a passing comment that government units sometimes ignore unfunded liabilities.

The authors argue that plan assets should be valued at market value. Whatever the other merits may be, there is one major difficulty if bonds and other fixed income assets are always to be valued at market. Bond prices rise or fall in response to changing market interest levels. Consequently, if fixed-income assets are marked up or down in response to market conditions, so should the assumed interest rate or rates on which plan liabilities are valued. The authors briefly refer to the problem but catalogue it as something the actuaries should deal with. That is inadequate appreciation of the difficulty. Without a solution, the authors are insisting in effect that pension plan liabilities be valued on a basis inconsistent with the basis for valuing plan assets.

The authors recognize the significance of actuarial assumptions, but their prescription is that the actuary should be required to share his responsibilities in that area with the employer and the accountant —the matter of assumptions should be "discussed" with them. There is nothing in their discussion which would lead one to conclude that such a mandate for discussions would produce any improvement in the state of affairs.

Statement by
C. L. Trowbridge, FSA
Bankers Life Company

Messrs. Hall and Landsittel have indeed been innovative in their work entitled "A New Look at the Accounting for Pension Costs." Whether they have been sufficiently persuasive to carry their readers to their conclusions depends upon whether they can sell their concepts with respect to the reality of pension "liabilities." If they are here successful, it would seem to this writer that their other conclusions follow. On the other hand, if pension plans of the defined benefit type have no such liabilities, then the whole framework falls. If this is the case, the two authors have merely led us in an exercise as to where a fallacious premise leads.

As will become clearer, this writer does not accept the Hall-Landsittel pension liability concept, and therefore reaches conclusions almost exactly opposite those of the two accountant-authors. He nonetheless commends the authors on the courage of their convictions, and on the doggedness with which they carry these convictions forward. The appearance of this work points out to actuaries and accountants that traditional thinking can be challenged. It is perhaps well that it can. It sharpens our thinking to examine a well expressed position, especially one we consider mistaken.

The remainder of this discussion will be a refutation of the Hall-Landsittel thesis, first on theoretical grounds, second by examining the practical aspects of pension funding and accounting problems. Finally there will be some remarks aimed at bringing the thinking of accountants and actuaries more closely together. Any tendency for these two professions to go separate ways in pension matters cannot be in the public interest.

Hall and Landsittel's basic premise is not clearly stated on any one page or in any single paragraph. It nonetheless runs through the entire work. The authors emphasize the undisputed fact that an employer assumes certain obligations when he undertakes or liberalizes a defined benefit pension plan; then claim that these obligations are properly accounted for by setting up a liability on the employer's balance sheet. This liability according to Hall and Landsittel is definable, and, within the limitations on any estimating process, quantifiable. The authors undertake the definition, and then leave to the actuarial profession the task of making the calculations based on appropriate actuarial assumptions.

The conclusions that the authors reach with respect to pension plan accounting are straightforward, once the premise is established. The liability goes on the employer's balance sheet. It should perhaps be noted that the liability item recommended for the employer's balance sheet is actually the net of a specially defined "present value of benefits earned to date" and the current value of pension fund assets. The books of the plan are symmetric to the books of the employer, indicating a plan liability (after offsetting assets) of the same amount as appears on the books of the employer (or employers) contributing to the plan. The employer's pension expense, in any accounting period (the period in which the plan is established or liberalized may or may not be an exception), is the amount that the employer contributes in that period, adjusted for the change in the liability.

The basic question that must be faced head-on is whether a defined benefit pension plan gives rise to employer "obligations" that have the nature (or the stature) of balance sheet liabilities. It is not really a question as whether such obligations exist, for of course they do. There are many kinds of obligations in the business world, only a few of which give rise to balance sheet liabilities.

Hall and Landsittel, perhaps inadvertently, have given their readers some help in deciding whether obligations are also liabilities. They attempt a definition of "hard" assets (those that are economic resources) as opposed to "soft" ones (that are not). For an asset to be properly shown on the balance sheet, Hall and Landsittel require that the asset meet three tests, those of utility, scarcity, and exchangeability. They conclude that pension assets in the nature of deferred charges do not meet these tests; and as soft assets have no place on the employer's balance sheet.

It is surprising to this writer that the two authors do not recognize the symmetry between assets and liabilities. Each can be considered the negative manifestation of the other. One business entity's liability is, generally speaking, another's asset. It would seem appropriate, therefore, to judge pension plan obligations by the same three tests —utility, scarcity, and exchangeability. In the eyes of this writer, pension plan obligations fail this hardness test for the same reasons as given by Hall and Landsittel for certain kinds of pension assets, and therefore should not appear on the employer's balance sheet.

Another way to view the matter is "what obligation did the employer *intend* to undertake when he established or liberalized his plan?" It is very clear from even a casual reading of pension literature or a study of pension plan documentation that employers have the understanding their commitments at any time are limited to the amounts already contributed. The Hall-Landsittel viewpoint is directly contrary to this prevalent employer understanding. It follows that employers must have been trapped; that they did not intend to create liabilities, and in fact went to some pains to see that they didn't, but did so in spite of themselves. This of course could be true, and some parts of the ERISA legislation make us wonder; but surely the matter of intent and common understanding must play a role in the appropriate accounting for pension plans.

Another way of approaching the "is there a liability" question has been suggested by the authors. They study the differences between (1) defined benefit pension plans, and (2) defined contribution plans of various types, coming to the conclusion that the two are inherently different with respect to "who is on the risk." Hall and Landsittel consider these differences great enough to justify radically different accounting treatment of the two plan types.

This writer is perfectly aware of the technical differences between defined benefit and defined contribution plans; but the more he studies employee benefit plans in general, the more he is impressed by the similarities between defined benefit and defined contribution plans. As an illustration of their essential similarity, consider this imaginary employer explanation of a plan he has recently adopted.

> By adopting this plan we have undertaken to contribute to a trustee in behalf of you employees; and we have arranged that the fund so set up will provide benefits for you and your dependents. We would like to be much more specific about *both* our contributions in your behalf and the benefits you will enjoy—but we find that we can be more specific about one or the other, but not both. After careful study involving both employer and employee viewpoints, it has been determined that it is better to be relatively specific about benefits and rather vague about employer contributions. We can give you *some* idea about the contributions we expect to make, but the contributions must be whatever they turn out to be, depending heavily on future events over which we have no control. To be absolutely straightforward, we must tell you that even your benefits entail a large measure of uncertainty. It is entirely necessary that we reserve the right to modify the plan, or even to terminate it entirely. While we have adopted this plan in good faith, and hope that we will be

able to carry out all of the obligations we have undertaken, neither benefits nor employer contributions are fixed forever. We would like to be able to remove your uncertainty, but both you and we must recognize that this cannot be.

Of course the reader appreciates that the reversal of the words "benefits" and "employer contributions" in the above changes the description from that of a defined benefit plan to one of the defined contribution type. Perhaps he also recognizes (as do Hall and Landsittel) that the two types blur at the margins, such that it is not always apparent which type-name is the more appropriate. Add to these considerations the substitutability of one type for the other, since their general objectives are the same. All of these concepts convince this writer that different accounting for the two types, based on differences not really that important, would lead to the biasing of what should be a free choice as between these competing types. It is hard to imagine an employer in his right mind adopting a defined-benefit plan if the Hall-Landsittel accounting were required.

Readers who are attracted to the argument presented in these last few paragraphs will wonder why Hall and Landsittel have taken the opposite view. This writer does not know the answer to this natural question, although he has carefully read what these authors have to say. He gets the impression from page 71 that these accountants have been misled by the terminology which has been employed (by actuaries and others) in describing the pension funding process. The noun "liability" appears very often in pension actuarial literature, though actuaries have never intended this word in the accounting sense. To imply otherwise exhibits a basic misunderstanding of the facts. Recognizing that they may have inadvertently led the public astray by their choice of words, actuaries have recently moved toward abandoning the liability terminology.

Up to this point this discussion has focused on the writer's belief that pension obligations are not "hard enough" to warrant their being on the employer's balance sheet. Concentration has so far been upon the more theoretical aspects. It is a test of theory, however, to see how it fits into the real world. Hall and Landsittel argue that, if the theory is sound, the fact that an accounting practice might have poor consequences should have little bearing. This writer tends to be theoretically oriented, and therefore is inclined to adopt this part of the authors' position; but he is practical enough to realize that if the consequences appear ridiculous it is high time to take a hard look at the theory.

There are several consequences of the Hall-Landsittel theory that need to be examined. The first of these is the pension obligation itself. If treated as "hard," the resulting liability, when it first appears on the balance sheet, adds to liabilities and directly reduces net worth. The magnitude of the liability thereby created (with no offsetting asset) can be enormous, especially in a service (or otherwise labor intensive) industry. It is easily conceivable that net worth might be eliminated entirely, causing technical bankruptcy. It would be indeed ironic if such bankruptcy were to cause plan cessation; then revaluation of the liability on a plan termination (instead of a going concern) basis were to make the employer solvent once again. To avoid such a ridiculous result, it seems likely that pension obligations, even in the Hall-Landsittel view, might be considered as "soft" for purposes of determining solvency. If so, the question remains as to why they were ever viewed as "hard."

Another consequence of the hard liability viewpoint is that the pension liability, and hence the net worth, varies widely from period to period due to actuarial gains and losses. Any deviation of experience from that assumed would have an upward effect on the liability if the experience were less "favorable" or a downward effect if it were more so. Contrary to the impression that one might gain from certain parts of the authors' work, actuarial gain or loss is not dominated by what goes on in the value of plan assets. Potentially more powerful are the effects of fluctuations in mortality, withdrawal, and salary levels. The net worth of the enterprise would be subject to the whims of chance to a degree that no one (including the auditors) could accept.

It should not be a surprise to the accountant-authors that their proposals have the effect of forcing the pension expense item for an accounting period to be the difference between the gross liability (liability before deduction of pension assets) at the period's beginning and its end, plus any investment loss, or less any investment gain. Because the two present values are jumpy as experience fluctuates, their difference is even more sensitive. The operating statement can therefore vary without apparent reason; in fact it can be expected to do so unless all effects of actuarial gain or loss are isolated from operating results. Hall and Landsittel suggest special treatment for gain or loss arising from the investment element, but do not seem to have considered similar treatment for other kinds of actuarial gain or loss which in many cases will be of much greater magnitude. Such treatment would have the characteristics and the objectives of the spreading techniques which the authors seem to dislike.

As a matter of fact, the authors' approach is really a throwback to the balance sheet reserve approach that was semipopular in earlier days. Under this approach it makes very little difference (on the employer's books) whether there is funding or not. Payment of a pension contribution to a trustee changes a hard asset (cash) into an offset against a soft liability, but otherwise does not affect the employer's books in any way. In fact the only effect of funding on the employer's operating statement is that the fluctuation in the value of the pension fund assets is one more variable that the operating statement must absorb (or be shielded from if some "nonrecurring" identification is used).

Up to this point this discussion has avoided the more technical of the issues raised by Hall and Landsittel. It would be preferable to continue on that basis; but there is one technical matter that cannot be overlooked. I refer to the matter only briefly mentioned earlier, which is pointed up by asking the question: "Assuming that it were appropriate to set up a hard pension liability, how would you define it?" Hall and Landsittel have recognized the importance of this question, and have had the courage to face it. Given the difficulty of the task, and especially the compromises that must be made between differing viewpoints, this writer thinks they have done reasonably well. Even so, all is not easy even on this front, and the reasons they give for their choice are not convincing.

The crux of their dilemma is that they would like to recognize two principles at the same time; but the two are inconsistent. They express the idea that the liability must have a flavor of "present value of pension earned to date." They would also like to have the pension accrual closely related to the payroll for that year, on the perfectly defensible theory that it is payroll that gives rise to pension benefits.

The authors discuss two alternative methods. One of these, the one that is ultimately discarded, will be recognized by actuaries as the entry-age normal concept applied with costs expressed as a level percent of the worker's pay. This fits the concept that pension expense should have a close connection with compensation. It is our surmise that the authors would have opted for this definition of the pension liability if it could have been better tied to the "pension earned to date" idea.

The actuarial cost method that clearly has the "pension already earned" concept is what this writer has called the traditional form of the accrued benefit cost method. It should be the choice for establishing any pension liability if it is intended that the measure of the liability is the present value of benefits already accrued (earned).

But the choice of Messrs. Hall and Landsittel is not the traditional form of the accrued benefit method. Instead it sets up a liability equal to the present value of benefits already accrued, where the timing of benefit accruals is determined *not by the plan* (more accurately the employee withdrawal provisions thereof), but instead by a definition that imposes the condition that the yearly benefit accrual shall be level as a percent of the individual's pay. Actuaries familiar with the writings of Professors Dan McGill and Howard Winklevoss will recognize this variation of the accrued benefit cost method.

Presumably this writer will not be asked how he would define the pension liability, because he is clearly on record as not believing in any. If he were forced to choose, he would probably opt for the traditional accrued benefit approach, on the assumption that if there has to be a liability, this one has the best rationale. He could not then claim any correlation with the individual's compensation to date, unless the terms of the plan then under examination just happened to define benefits accrued to date in the Hall-Landsittel fashion. This would be likely only on a plan whose benefit formula was of the salary-service type, with benefits based on career pay. These plans are becoming less common rather than more so, so the Hall-Landsittel definition of benefits earned to date is not a natural one.

This brings this discussion to the final point, that having to do with the respective roles of actuaries and accountants in pension matters. The Hall-Landsittel view appears to be that pension funding and pension accounting are separate and distinct; that the actuary should influence one and the accountant the other; and that, if there is *any* relationship between the accounting and funding phases of the pension problem, the relationship is similar to that between cash and accrual methods of accounting.

This writer's view is quite different. He considers the resolution of pension accounting problems as one of the two prime reasons why pension funding takes place (the security of employee pension expectations being the other). In choosing the actuarial cost method that determines to a large extent the employer's funding pattern for the year, the actuary should (and does) consider whether the resulting employer contribution is an appropriate charge against the operations for that accounting period. Assuming the actuary *and the accountant* can conscientiously recommend that contribution as an appropriate accounting charge, each should resist the employer's changing the contribution for tax or cash flow reasons. An asset or liability should be set up on the employer's books only if the employer chooses not to accept the recommendation, and then only to make the pension accrual for the period a sensible one. If this view is adopted, there need be few instances indeed where cash and accrual accounting for pension items differ, and no reason whatsoever for the actuarial and the accounting views to be different.

In short, the actuary and the accountant have a community of interest based on similar objectives. Both want the employer's accounting and the pension funding to reflect as best it can the "true" cost of the pension plan for the current period. Actuaries and accountants, as responsible professionals, must realize that their efforts complement each other. Only if it is fully recognized that pension accounting and pension funding are only slightly different phases of the same basic problem can progress occur. It is therefore up to the two professions to learn from each other; and to see that their efforts are coordinated such that their common employer-client operates intelligently in what must always be a difficult area.

Statement by
Howard E. Winklevoss
Associate Professor
The Wharton School

Messrs. Hall and Landsittel have indeed presented us with a new look at accounting for pension costs. Their approach represents a significant departure from previous treatments of the subject and only time will tell whether their concepts will take hold. The purpose of this discussion is not to present my views of the Hall-Landsittel approach to accounting for pension costs, but rather, to compare their procedures for establishing the plan's liability and annual cost to the liability and annual cost under several other actuarial cost methods currently being used with pension plans. This comparison may be helpful to readers in evaluating the merits of the Hall-Landsittel approach.

Generic Actuarial Cost Methods

There are numerous actuarial cost methods in current use that develop a different normal cost and actuarial liability for the same underlying data and actuarial assumptions.[1] Nevertheless, all cost methods can be characterized as belonging either to the family of *accured benefit cost methods* or the family of *projected benefit cost methods*.

The normal cost under the accrued benefit cost methods is equal to the present value of the benefits assumed to be earned by the employee for his current year of service. In other words, the normal cost is equal to the dollar value that would be required today to fully fund the benefit assumed to be earned by the employee in the current year. The actuarial liability under these methods is equal to the present value of the *cumulative benefits* allocated to the employee up to the year in question.

---

[1] The *normal cost* of an actuarial cost method is the annual cost that, if made from the employee's entry age to his retirement age, will fully account for the cost of his pension, provided there are no plan changes and that all actuarial assumptions are met. If these conditions are not met, or if the plan is started during the employee's working career, a supplemental cost will be generated to account for these factors. Since the authors recommend that any unfunded supplemental liability be charged to the current year, this discussion need only deal with each cost method's normal cost. The *actuarial liability* of a cost method can be viewed, either as the cumulative normal cost of an employee, or as the difference between the present value of his future benefits and the present value of his future normal costs.

Projected benefit cost methods ignore the current and cumulative benefits associated with the employee and deal instead with his projected (retirement-date) benefit. The objective of these methods is to spread the cost of the projected benefit on a level basis throughout the employee's career, either as a level annual dollar amount or as a level annual percentage of salary. The actuarial liability of the projected benefit cost methods is nothing more than an actuarial identity, having no relationship to the cumulative benefits associated with the employee. In particular, the actuarial liability is equal to the employee's total liability (present value of his projected benefit) less that portion of the total liability yet to be accounted for by future level costs (i.e., the present value of future normal costs).

The projected benefit cost methods are more common than the accrued benefit cost methods, both for accounting and funding purposes, but a noticeable trend towards the use of the accrued benefit cost methods has developed in recent years.[2] The fact that Hall and Landsittel in effect recommend the use of an accrued benefit cost method for pension accounting will undoubtedly create additional interest in these methods.

One of the principal reasons, but by no means the sole reason, for the lack of popularity of the accrued benefit cost methods is the plain fact that final average salary plans, which are becoming quite popular, do not have a definitely determinable benefit for each year of the employee's service. As noted earlier, the accrued benefit cost methods require a benefit to be associated with each year of service for deriving a normal cost, and the cumulative benefits are used in deriving the actuarial liability. Nevertheless, there are at least three logical ways to derive a year-to-year benefit for use with the accrued benefit cost methods when the plan has a final average benefit formula.

1.   Apply the plan benefit formula both to this year's and next year's current salary average and service. The *difference* between the two benefits so derived is the benefit assumed to accrue in the current year.

2.   Apply the plan benefit formula to the employee's expected final average salary and service at retirement, and allocate the projected benefit so derived to each year of service in amounts that equal a *constant percentage of salary* at each age.

---

[2] This author and his colleague, Dr. Dan M. McGill, may be partially responsible for this trend, having written an article several years ago that analyzed the advantages of such methods under some circumstances. See Dan M. McGill and Howard E. Winklevoss, "A Quantitative Analysis of Actuarial Cost Methods for Pension Plans," *Conference of Actuaries in Public Practice*, vol. 23, 1974, pp. 212–76.

3. Same as version (2), but allocate the projected benefit to each year of service in *equal dollar amounts.*

Although Messrs. Hall and Landsittel do not explicitly state the fact, they end up recommending the second version given above (prorating the projected benefit by salary) for use with the accrued benefit cost methods. Thus, the annual accounting cost, ignoring actuarial gains and losses, plan amendments, and past service liabilities, under their approach is the present value of the benefits so allocated to the employee's current year of service. Similarly, the liability recommended by the authors is the present value of the *cumulative* benefits allocated to the employee up to the year of valuation.

The remaining portion of this discussion is devoted to comparing the author's recommended version of the accrued benefit cost method to the other two versions of this method as described above, and to two versions of the family of projected benefit cost methods.[3] The material used in the following sections is based on a book written by this author and entitled *Pension Mathematics: With Numerical Illustrations*, which will be published by the Pension Research Council in January, 1977.

Cost Methods Compared

Five actuarial cost methods, three of which are accrued benefit cost methods, and two of which are projected benefit cost methods, are compared in this discussion. The names of these methods, along with their identifying symbols, are given below:

ABCM—Accrued Benefit Cost Method, where the annual benefits are equal to the difference between the benefits derived from applying the benefit formula to this year's and next year's current salary average and years of service (version #1 above).

^{CS}ABCM—Accrued Benefit Cost Method with the projected benefit prorated by salary, i.e., each year's benefit allocation is a Constant percentage of Salary (version #2 above).

^{CA}ABCM—Accrued Benefit Cost Method with the projected benefit prorated by service, i.e., each year's benefit allocation is a Constant dollar Amount (version #3 above).

---

[3] There are several other versions of the projected benefit cost method not considered here; however, the two versions studied produce results similar to these other variations of the projected benefit cost method.

CSPBCM—Projected Benefit Cost Method, where the normal cost is derived to be a Constant percentage of Salary (also known as the Entry Age Normal Cost Method with level-percentage-of-salary normal costs).

CAPBCM—Projected Benefit Cost Method, where the normal cost is derived to be a Constant dollar Amount (also known as the Entry Age Normal Cost Method with level dollar normal costs).

Assumptions

The following assumptions underlie the numerical comparisons.

Benefit Formula. 1½ percent of final 5 year average salary per year of service.

Ancillary Benefits. None.

Mortality Rates. 1971 Group Annuity Mortality Table.

Termination Rates. Select and ultimate schedule, with what might be considered *medium* rates.

Disability Rates. Typical rates assumed.

Retirement Rates. 100 percent at age 65.

Salary Rates. 7 percent (approx.), consisting of a merit scale (approximately 2 percent), 4 percent inflation, and 1 percent productivity.

Interest Rate. 7 percent, consisting of 2 percent pure rate, 4 percent inflation, and 1 percent risk premium.

These assumptions are believed to be somewhat more typical than the assumptions used by Hall and Landsittel in their numerical illustrations.

Comparison of Benefit Allocations

Figure 1 shows the percentage of an employee's projected benefit allocated to each age, from his entry age 30 to his retirement age 65, under the five actuarial cost methods. The CAABCM develops a straight line, indicating that a constant proportion of the projected benefit is allocated under this method. The ABCM and CSABCM develop increasing patterns of benefit allocations. The pattern under the CSABCM represent a constant proportion of the employee's salary at each age, which necessarily increases in dollar amounts throughout the employee's working career. The allocation pattern under the ABCM is somewhat lower at the younger ages and somewhat higher at the older ages than the pattern under the ^{CS}ABCM.

It was pointed out earlier that the projected benefit cost methods are not based on benefit accruals. Nevertheless, it is possible to derive the portion of the employee's projected benefit implicitly allocated to each age by determining the benefit that each year's normal cost would fully fund.

The ^{CS}PBCM, which has a normal cost equal to a level percentage of salary, develops a decreasing pattern of benefit accruals, beginning at 8 percent of the projected benefit for age 30 and ending at 1 percent by age 64. The ^{CA}PBCM, like its sister method, also develops a decreasing benefit allocation pattern, beginning with 16 percent of the projected benefit allocated to age 30 and ending with a small fraction of 1 percent at age 64.

Based on the benefit allocation patterns shown in Figure 1, one might conclude that the accrued benefit cost methods develop rational patterns of benefit allocation, whereas the projected benefit cost methods do not. In fact, the projected benefit cost methods end up allocating the employee's projected benefit in exactly the opposite manner in which the projected benefit is earned, with the largest allocation near the employee's entry age and the smallest allocation near his retirement age.

FIGURE 1

Percentage of Projected Retirement Benefit Allocated to Each Age under Various Actuarial Cost Methods

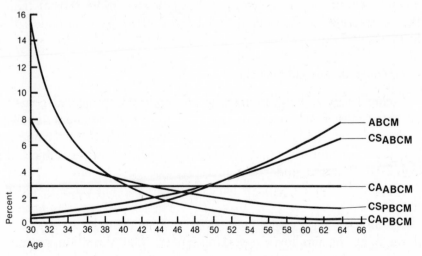

It is not clear which version of the accrued benefit cost method is the *most* rational. Hall and Landsittel argue that the ᶜˢABCM is the most rational approach in that salary represents the best measure of the employee's productivity to the firm; hence, the projected benefit should be spread accordingly. Others would argue that the ABCM is the most rational in that it generates benefit accruals by following the specific provisions of the plan. Still, others would opt for the ᶜᴬABCM inasmuch as it spreads the projected benefit out evenly over the employee's career.

Figure 2 shows the employee's *cumulative* benefits allocated up to each age, again expressed as a percentage of his projected benefit, under the five actuarial cost methods. An employee's cumulative benefits, it will be recalled, are used in determining each cost method's actuarial liability, a procedure also applicable to the projected benefit cost methods if the cumulative benefits are developed from the benefit allocations of Figure 1.

FIGURE 2

Cumulative Percentage of Projected Retirement Benefit Allocated to Each Age under Various Actuarial Cost Methods

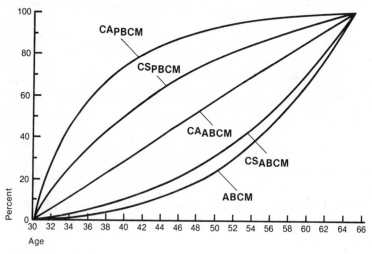

The ᶜᴬABCM has a linear benefit accumulation. The ABCM and ᶜˢABCM have lower benefit accumulations and the ᶜˢPBCM and ᶜᴬPBCM have higher benefit accumulations than the accumulations of the ᶜᴬABCM. It is significant that 50 percent of the employee's projected benefit is allocated by the midpoint of the employee's career under the ᶜᴬABCM. The 50 percent benchmark is reached approximately three-fourths of the way through the employee's career under the ABCM and ᶜˢABCM, and is reached during the first quarter of the employee's career under the projected benefit cost methods.

Comparison of Normal Cost and Actuarial Liability

Figure 3 shows the normal cost as a percentage of the employee's salary from his entry age to his retirement age under the five actuarial cost methods. The normal cost in each case is found by determining

FIGURE 3

Normal Cost as a Percentage of Salary under Various Actuarial Cost Methods

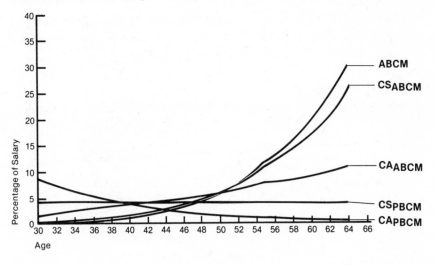

the present value of the benefits allocated to each age as shown in Figure 1.

The ᶜˢPBCM develops a straight line, indicating that costs represent a level percentage of salary. In this illustration, the ᶜˢPBCM normal cost is about 5 percent of salary. The ᶜᴬPBCM develops a decreasing cost pattern, reflecting the fact that this method has a level dollar normal cost which would naturally represent a decreasing percentage of salary.

The ᶜᴬABCM has an increasing normal cost pattern, beginning at 2 percent of salary during age 30 and ending at 10 percent by age 64. The most striking cost patterns in Figure 3 are those of the ABCM and ᶜˢABCM, both of which increase sharply as a percentage of salary throughout the employee's career. The normal costs under these methods are 25 to 30 percent of salary by age 64.

If one were to analyze the rationality of the normal cost as given in Figure 3, he might come to the exact opposite conclusions from those reached by inspecting the benefit allocations of each cost method. The projected benefit cost methods, and particularly the csPBCM, appear to develop rational cost patterns, whereas the cost patterns under the accrued benefit cost methods appear to be ir-

FIGURE 4

Actuarial Liability as a Percentage of Salary under Various Actuarial Cost Methods

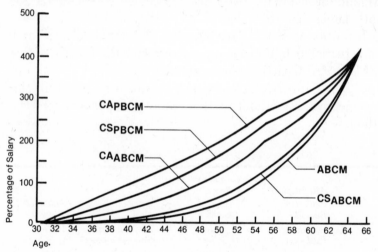

rational. In the latter case, a disproportionate amount of the pension costs is allocated over the last portion of the employee's working career.

Figure 4 shows the actuarial liability as a percentage of salary under the five actuarial cost methods. This liability, it should be noted, is determined by calculating the present value of the cumulative benefits allocated at each age as shown in Figure 2. This is, of course, the basic definition of the actuarial liability for the accrued benefit cost methods, but it is applicable also to the projected benefit cost methods when the benefits are determined as they are in Figure 2.

All methods have the same actuarial liability at the employee's entry age (equal to zero) and at his retirement age (equal to the present value of his benefit at that age). The actuarial liabilities at the intermediate ages, however, differ significantly, as measured by the vertical distance between the actuarial liability curves.

The ABCM and ^{CS}ABCM develop the lowest actuarial liabilities; the ^{CA}ABCM develops an intermediate actuarial liability; and the two projected benefit cost methods develop the largest actuarial liabilities. If indeed the ABCM and the ^{CS}ABCM generate liabilities most closely associated with the employee's accrued benefits under the final average salary plan, then the actuarial liabilities under the ^{CA}ABCM, and especially the two projected benefit cost methods, are significantly larger than the liabilities for accrued benefits throughout most of his working career. In assessing the rationality of each method's actuarial liability, one would undoubtedly conclude that the ABCM or ^{CS}ABCM is the most rational.

Figure 5 is a summary of the degree of rationality, based on this author's subjective evaluation, of the various components for each cost method.

FIGURE 5

	Allocation of Projected Benefit	Cumulative Allocation of Projected Benefit	Normal Cost	Actuarial Liability
ABCM............	Rational	Rational	Not rational	Rational
^{CS}ABCM........	Rational	Rational	Not rational	Rational
^{CA}ABCM........	Reasonably rational	Reasonably rational	Reasonably rational	Reasonably rational
^{CS}PBCM........	Not rational	Not rational	Rational	Not rational
^{CA}PBCM........	Not rational	Not rational	Rational	Not rational

The ABCM and ^{CS}ABCM are found to be rational in terms of the allocation of the projected benefit, the cumulative allocation of the projected benefits, and the actuarial liability, but not in terms of the normal cost. Exactly the reverse is found for the projected benefit cost methods. Consequently, selecting among these cost methods must rest with the importance attached to these various factors. Hall and Landsittel favor the accrued benefit cost methods, and in particular the ^{CS}ABCM, while most actuaries, and undoubtedly most accountants, have traditionally opted for projected benefit cost methods.

The ^{CA}ABCM is rated in Figure 5 as being reasonably rational on all points. It tends to develop benefit allocations, cumulative benefit allocations, normal costs, and actuarial liabilities that fall between the extreme of the other cost methods. Some might argue that this method is not rational on *any* factor, while others might argue that it strikes a meaningful balance between the rational and irrational aspects of the other four cost methods. In the final analysis, each reader will have to come to his own conclusions, since such evaluations inevitably involve one's subjective viewpoints.

Plan Comparisons

Up to this point the comparison of the five actuarial cost methods has been based on a single employee. This is sometimes a treacherous undertaking, since a pension plan consists of a group of employees and the normal cost pattern and actuarial liability for the plan as a whole may not conform to the patterns for a single employee. While it is true that individual employees within the plan population will have normal cost and actuarial liability patterns like those presented earlier, the flow of new employees into the population requires one to analyze the *average* normal cost and actuarial liability pattern among all employees over time. The conclusions for the entire plan may or may not conform to the conclusions based on one plan participant.

In this section, a hypothetical plan population is simulated over a period of 50 years and used as the basis to compare cost methods. Characteristics of the population during each year of the simulation are given in Table 1. The population begins with a relatively young average age and service (age 34.5 and 4.6 years of service). The population grows to double its original size after 25 years, at which point its average age is 39.5 and its average service is 9.2 years. Beyond the twenty-fifth year, the population decreases and by the end of the 50 years it attains the same size as it was in the first year. In the fiftieth year of the simulation, the population has an average age of 45.9 and an average years of service of 16.0.

The reason the population is simulated according to the above increasing and then decreasing growth pattern is to compare the cost methods under the conditions of (1) an extremely young and growing labor force, (2) a relatively stable, intermediate labor force in terms of age and service, and (3) an extremely old and declining labor force. These variations are important when analyzing the effects of different cost methods, since each method reacts differently to various plan populations.

TABLE 1

Population Statistics

| Year | Active Employees | | | Nonactive Employees as % of Actives | | | |
	Number as % of Initial Size	Average Age	Average Service	Retired	Vested Terminated	Disabled	Surviving Spouses
0.........	100.0	34.9	4.6	0.0	0.0	0.0	0.0
1.........	107.8	35.0	4.8	0.3	0.7	0.0	0.0
2.........	115.4	35.1	4.9	0.7	1.4	0.0	0.0
3.........	122.6	35.3	5.1	1.0	2.0	0.1	0.0
4.........	129.4	35.5	5.2	1.3	2.7	0.1	0.0
5.........	136.0	35.7	5.4	1.6	3.4	0.1	0.0
6.........	142.2	35.9	5.6	1.9	4.1	0.1	0.0
7.........	148.2	36.1	5.8	2.2	4.8	0.1	0.0
8.........	153.8	36.3	6.0	2.6	5.5	0.2	0.1
9.........	159.0	36.5	6.2	2.9	6.3	0.2	0.1
10.........	164.0	36.7	6.4	3.2	7.1	0.2	0.1
11.........	168.6	37.0	6.6	3.6	7.9	0.3	0.1
12.........	173.0	37.2	6.8	4.0	8.8	0.3	0.1
13.........	177.0	37.4	7.0	4.3	9.7	0.4	0.1
14.........	180.6	37.6	7.2	4.7	10.6	0.4	0.2
15.........	184.0	37.7	7.4	5.1	11.6	0.4	0.2
16.........	187.0	37.9	7.6	5.5	12.6	0.5	0.2
17.........	189.8	38.1	7.7	6.0	13.6	0.5	0.2
18.........	192.2	38.3	7.9	6.4	14.7	0.6	0.3
19.........	194.2	38.5	8.1	6.9	15.8	0.7	0.3
20.........	196.0	38.7	8.3	7.4	16.9	0.7	0.3
21.........	197.4	38.8	8.5	7.8	18.0	0.8	0.4
22.........	198.6	39.0	8.7	8.4	19.2	0.9	0.4
23.........	199.4	39.2	8.8	8.9	20.4	0.9	0.5
24.........	199.8	39.3	9.0	9.4	21.6	1.0	0.5
25.........	200.0	39.5	9.2	10.0	22.9	1.1	0.6
26.........	199.8	39.7	9.4	10.6	24.1	1.2	0.6
27.........	199.4	39.8	9.5	11.2	25.4	1.2	0.7
28.........	198.6	40.0	9.7	11.8	26.8	1.3	0.8
29.........	197.4	40.1	9.9	12.4	28.2	1.4	0.8
30.........	196.0	40.3	10.1	13.1	29.6	1.5	0.9
31.........	194.2	40.4	10.2	13.8	31.1	1.6	1.0
32.........	192.2	40.6	10.4	14.6	32.6	1.7	1.1
33.........	189.8	40.8	10.6	15.3	34.1	1.8	1.1
34.........	187.0	40.9	10.8	16.1	35.8	1.9	1.2
35.........	184.0	41.1	10.9	17.0	37.5	2.1	1.3
36.........	180.6	41.3	11.1	17.9	39.2	2.2	1.4
37.........	177.0	41.4	11.3	18.8	41.1	2.3	1.5
38.........	173.0	41.6	11.5	19.8	43.0	2.4	1.7
39.........	168.6	41.8	11.7	20.9	45.1	2.6	1.8
40.........	164.0	42.0	12.0	22.0	47.3	2.7	1.9
41.........	159.0	42.3	12.2	23.2	49.7	2.9	2.1
42.........	153.8	42.5	12.4	24.5	52.2	3.0	2.2
43.........	148.2	42.8	12.7	25.9	54.9	3.2	2.4
44.........	142.2	43.1	13.0	27.4	57.9	3.4	2.5
45.........	136.0	43.4	13.4	29.1	61.2	3.6	2.7
46.........	129.4	43.7	13.8	30.9	64.9	3.9	3.0
47.........	122.6	44.2	14.2	33.0	69.0	4.2	3.2
48.........	115.4	44.6	14.7	35.3	73.7	4.5	3.5
49.........	107.8	45.2	15.3	38.1	79.1	4.8	3.8
50.........	100.0	45.9	16.0	41.2	85.4	5.2	4.2
Mature Population...		40.2	10.1	22.2	46.1	2.7	2.3

Table 1 also shows the number of retired, vested terminated, disabled and surviving spouse plan members, each expressed as a percentage of the number of active employees. The actuarial assumptions underlying the population simulation and other analyses in this section are identical to those given earlier. In addition, ancillary benefits are assumed as follows:

Vesting.   Full vesting after 10 years of service.

Disability.   50 percent of accrued benefits (as defined by applying the plan benefit formula to the current salary and service) if disability occurs after age 40 and 15 years of service

Death.   50 percent spouses benefit payable for the life of the surviving spouse if death occurs after age 55 with 20 years of service

Normal Cost Comparison.   Table 2 gives the plan normal cost under the five actuarial cost methods. The pay-as-you-go costs are also given in column one for comparison purposes. The ABCM and ^{CS}ABCM develop cost patterns that increase fairly sharply over time, beginning at about 3 percent of salary in the first year of the simulation and ending at about 10 percent in the fiftieth year. The ^{CA}ABCM develops moderately increasing costs, beginning at 5 percent and increasing to 7 percent. As expected, the ^{CS}PBCM develops a nearly perfectly level cost pattern, beginning at 5.8 percent and decreasing to 5.7 percent of salary. Finally, the ^{CA}PBCM shows a decreasing cost pattern, with a value of 7.2 percent in the first year, scaling downward to 3.6 percent in the last year.

Table 2 points out that, for the plan as a whole, the increasing cost pattern of the accrued benefit cost methods and the decreasing cost pattern of the ^{CA}PBCM are not nearly as sharp for the plan as a whole as they were found to be for an individual plan participant.

The ^{CS}PBCM still develops the most rational cost pattern, followed by the ^{CA}ABCM and the ^{CA}PBCM. The ABCM and ^{CS}ABCM still have the least rational cost pattern, but one that appears to be far more rational than the pattern for a single employee.

Actuarial Liability Comparison.   Table 3 shows the actuarial liability under each method as a percentage of the Termination-of-Plan Liability (TPL).[4] The TPL is used as a benchmark because it is a liability measure independent of a given actuarial most method.

---

[4] The TPL is the liability of the plan that would exist if it were to be terminated in the year in question. It is based on the 1971 Group Annuity Mortality Table and a 7 percent interest rate.

TABLE 2

Normal Cost as a Percentage of Salary under Various Actuarial Cost Methods

Year	Pay As You Go	$ABCM$	$^{cs}ABCM$	$^{cA}ABCM$	$^{cs}PBCM$	$^{cA}PBCM$
0	.0	2.7	3.3	4.9	5.8	7.2
1	.1	2.8	3.3	5.0	5.8	7.1
2	.1	2.9	3.4	5.0	5.8	7.1
3	.2	3.0	3.5	5.1	5.8	7.0
4	.3	3.1	3.6	5.1	5.8	6.9
5	.4	3.2	3.7	5.2	5.8	6.8
6	.4	3.3	3.8	5.2	5.8	6.8
7	.5	3.4	3.9	5.3	5.8	6.7
8	.6	3.6	4.0	5.3	5.8	6.6
9	.7	3.7	4.1	5.4	5.8	6.5
10	.8	3.8	4.2	5.4	5.8	6.5
11	.9	4.0	4.3	5.5	5.8	6.4
12	1.0	4.1	4.4	5.5	5.8	6.3
13	1.1	4.2	4.6	5.6	5.8	6.2
14	1.2	4.4	4.7	5.6	5.8	6.2
15	1.3	4.5	4.8	5.6	5.8	6.1
16	1.5	4.6	4.9	5.7	5.8	6.0
17	1.6	4.8	5.0	5.7	5.8	6.0
18	1.8	4.9	5.1	5.7	5.8	5.9
19	1.9	5.1	5.3	5.8	5.8	5.8
20	2.1	5.2	5.4	5.8	5.8	5.8
21	2.3	5.3	5.5	5.8	5.8	5.7
22	2.5	5.5	5.6	5.9	5.8	5.6
23	2.7	5.6	5.7	5.9	5.8	5.6
24	3.0	5.8	5.8	5.9	5.8	5.5
25	3.2	5.9	5.9	5.9	5.8	5.5
26	3.5	6.0	6.0	6.0	5.8	5.4
27	3.7	6.2	6.1	6.0	5.8	5.4
28	4.0	6.3	6.2	6.0	5.8	5.3
29	4.3	6.4	6.4	6.0	5.7	5.3
30	4.6	6.6	6.5	6.1	5.7	5.2
31	4.9	6.7	6.6	6.1	5.7	5.2
32	5.3	6.9	6.7	6.1	5.7	5.1
33	5.6	7.0	6.8	6.1	5.7	5.1
34	6.0	7.1	6.9	6.1	5.7	5.0
35	6.4	7.3	7.0	6.2	5.7	5.0
36	6.8	7.4	7.1	6.2	5.7	4.9
37	7.2	7.5	7.2	6.2	5.7	4.8
38	7.7	7.7	7.3	6.2	5.7	4.8
39	8.2	7.8	7.5	6.3	5.7	4.7
40	8.7	8.0	7.6	6.3	5.7	4.7
41	9.2	8.2	7.7	6.3	5.7	4.6
42	9.8	8.3	7.9	6.4	5.7	4.5
43	10.4	8.5	8.0	6.4	5.7	4.5
44	11.0	8.7	8.2	6.5	5.7	4.4
45	11.7	8.9	8.3	6.5	5.7	4.3
46	12.5	9.2	8.5	6.5	5.7	4.2
47	13.3	9.4	8.7	6.6	5.7	4.1
48	14.2	9.7	9.0	6.7	5.7	3.9
49	15.2	10.1	9.2	6.7	5.7	3.8
50	16.4	10.4	9.6	6.8	5.7	3.6
∞	9.7	6.9	6.7	6.0	5.7	5.2

TABLE 3

Actuarial Liability as a Percentage of the Termination-of-Plan Liability

$Year$	$ABCM$	$^{CS}ABCM$	$^{CA}ABCM$	$^{CS}PBCM$	$^{CA}PBCM$
0.........	97	134	256	335	465
1.........	98	132	245	316	435
2.........	98	131	236	302	410
3.........	99	130	229	290	390
4.........	99	128	223	279	373
5.........	99	127	218	270	359
6.........	100	127	213	262	345
7.........	100	126	209	255	333
8.........	100	125	205	249	323
9.........	100	125	201	243	312
10.........	101	124	198	237	303
11.........	101	123	194	231	294
12.........	101	123	191	226	286
13.........	101	122	188	222	278
14.........	101	122	186	217	271
15.........	101	121	183	213	264
16.........	102	121	180	208	257
17.........	102	120	178	205	251
18.........	102	120	175	201	245
19.........	102	119	173	197	239
20.........	102	119	171	194	234
21.........	102	118	168	190	229
22.........	102	118	166	187	224
23.........	102	117	164	184	219
24.........	102	117	162	182	215
25.........	102	116	161	179	211
26.........	102	116	159	176	207
27.........	102	115	157	174	203
28.........	102	115	155	172	200
29.........	102	115	154	169	196
30.........	102	114	152	167	193
31.........	102	114	151	165	190
32.........	102	114	149	163	187
33.........	102	113	148	161	184
34.........	102	113	147	160	182
35.........	102	113	146	158	179
36.........	102	112	144	156	177
37.........	102	112	143	155	175
38.........	102	112	142	153	172
39.........	102	111	141	152	170
40.........	102	111	140	150	168
41.........	102	111	139	149	166
42.........	102	111	138	148	165
43.........	102	110	137	147	163
44.........	102	110	136	145	161
45.........	102	110	136	144	159
46.........	102	110	135	143	158
47.........	102	110	134	142	156
48.........	102	109	133	141	154
49.........	102	109	132	140	153
50.........	101	109	132	139	151
∞	102	110	137	147	164

The ABCM and ^{CS}ABCM actuarial liabilities are the smallest; the ^{CS}PBCM and ^{CA}PBCM actuarial liabilities are the largest; and the ^{CA}ABCM actuarial liability falls between these extremes. It is a matter of judgment as to which of these liabilities is the most appropriate for use in pension plan accounting. Hall and Landsittel believe the ^{CS}ABCM liability is the most appropriate, although some may argue that the ABCM actuarial liability, which represents the value of accrued benefits as defined in the plan, is the more appropriate. Undoubtedly, few would argue that the actuarial liability under the projected benefit cost methods is an appropriate one, but this liability is a necessary consequence of the level cost pattern of these methods. While the ^{CA}ABCM actuarial liability is considerably larger than the ABCM, it does represent an intermediate value which some may find appealing, especially when viewed in terms of this method's reasonably level normal cost pattern.

Summary and Conclusions

It is difficult, if not impossible, to have the best of both worlds in one actuarial cost method. Those methods that develop level costs also develop distorted actuarial liabilities when viewed in terms of accrued benefits. By the same token, cost methods that develop rational actuarial liabilities generally develop increasing normal cost patterns. The ^{CA}ABCM might be viewed as either a cost method that has neither an appropriate normal cost pattern nor an appropriate actuarial liability, or as a method that mitigates the undesirable aspects of other cost methods. Hall and Landsittel reject the projected cost methods and select the ^{CS}ABCM as a means of establishing the plan's liability and costs. At least some readers will take exactly the opposite position. The results of this discussion may provide other readers with a compromise method; namely, the ^{CA}ABCM. Again, only time will tell which procedures will eventually dominate. Hopefully, this discussion will facilitate the deliberations to this end.

supplement A

Accounting Principles Board Opinion No. 8

Accounting for the Cost of Pension Plans

CONTENTS

INTRODUCTION

1. Pension plans have developed in an environment characterized by a complex array of social concepts and pressures, legal considerations, actuarial techniques, income tax laws and regulations, business philosophies, and accounting concepts and practices. Each plan reflects the interaction of the environment with the interests of the persons concerned with its design, interpretation and operation. From these factors have resulted widely divergent practices in accounting for the cost of pension plans.

2. An increased significance of pension cost in relation to the financial position and results of operations of many businesses has been brought about by the substantial growth of private pension plans, both in numbers of employees covered and in amounts of retirement benefits. The assets accumulated and the future benefits to employees under these plans have reached such magnitude that changes in actuarial assumptions concerning pension fund earnings, employee mortality and turnover, retirement age, etc., and the treatment of differences between such assumptions and actual experience, can have important effects on the pension cost recognized for accounting purposes from year to year.

3. In Accounting Research Bulletin No. 47, *Accounting for Costs of Pension Plans*, the committee on accounting procedure stated its preferences that "costs based on current and future services should be systematically accrued during the expected period of active service of the covered employees" and that "costs based on past services should be charged off over some reasonable period, provided the allocation is made on a systematic and rational basis and does not cause distortion of the operating results in any one year." In recognition of the divergent views then existing, however, the committee also said "as a minimum, the accounts and financial statement should reflect accruals which equal the present worth, actuarially calculated, of pension commitments to employees to the extent that pension rights have vested in the employees, reduced, in the case of the balance sheet, by any accumulated trusteed funds or annuity contracts purchased." The committee did not explain what was meant by the term "vested" and did not make any recommendations concerning appropriate actuarial cost methods or recognition of actuarial gains and losses.

4. Despite the issuance of Accounting Research Bulletin No. 47,

accounting for the cost of pension plans has varied widely among companies and has sometimes resulted in wide year-to-year fluctuations in the provisions for pension cost of a single company. Generally, companies have provided pension cost equivalent to the amounts paid to a pension fund or used to purchase annuities. In many cases such payments have included amortization of past service cost (and prior service cost arising on amendment of a plan) over periods ranging from about ten to forty years; in other cases the payments have not included amortization but have included an amount equivalent to interest (see definition of *interest* in the Glossary, Appendix B) on unfunded prior service cost. In some cases payments from year to year have varied with fluctuations in company earnings or with the availability of funds. In other cases payments have been affected by the Federal income tax rates in effect at a particular time. The recognition of actuarial gains and losses in the year of their determination, or intermittently, has also caused year-to-year variations in such payments.

5. Because of the increasing importance of pensions and the variations in accounting for them, the Accounting Principles Board authorized Accounting Research Study No. 8, *Accounting for the Cost of Pension Plans* (referred to hereinafter as the "Research Study"). The Research Study was published in May 1965 by the American Institute of Certified Public Accountants and has been widely distributed. The Board has carefully examined the recommendations of the Research Study and considered many comments and articles about it. The Board's conclusions agree in most respects with, but differ in some from, those in the Research Study.

6. The Board has concluded that this Opinion is needed to clarify the accounting principles and to narrow the practices applicable to accounting for the cost of pension plans. This Opinion supersedes Accounting Research Bulletin No. 43, Chapter 13, Section A, *Compensation: Pension Plans—Annuity Costs Based on Past Service* and Accounting Research Bulletin No. 47, *Accounting for Costs of Pension Plans.*

7. The computation of pension cost for accounting purposes requires the use of actuarial techniques and judgment. Generally pension cost should be determined from a study by an actuary, giving effect to the conclusions set forth in this Opinion. It should be noted that the actuarial cost methods and their application for accounting purposes may differ from those used for funding purposes.

A discussion of actuarial valuations, assumptions and cost methods is included in Appendix A. The terminology used in this Opinion to describe pension cost and actuarial cost methods is consistent with that generally used by actuaries and others concerned with pension plans. A Glossary of such terminology is included in Appendix B.

PENSION PLANS COVERED BY THIS OPINION

8. For the purposes of this Opinion, a pension plan is an arrangement whereby a company undertakes to provide its retired employees with benefits that can be determined or estimated in advance from the provisions of a document or documents or from the company's practices. Ordinarily, such benefits are monthly pension payments but, in many instances, they include death and disability payments. However, death and disability payments under a separate arrangement are not considered in this Opinion. The Opinion applies both to written plans and to plans whose existence may be implied from a well-defined, although perhaps unwritten, company policy. A company's practice of paying retirement benefits to selected employees in amounts determined on a case-by-case basis at or after retirement does not constitute a pension plan under this Opinion. The Opinion applies to pension cost incurred outside the United States under plans that are reasonably similar to those contemplated by this Opinion, when included in financial statements intended to conform with generally accepted accounting principles in the United States. The Opinion applies to unfunded plans as well as to insured plans and trust fund plans. It applies to defined-contribution plans as well as to defined-benefit plans. It applies also to deferred compensation contracts with individual employees if such contracts, taken together, are equivalent to a pension plan. It does not apply to deferred profit-sharing plans except to the extent that such a plan is, or is part of, an arrangement that is in substance a pension plan.

BASIC ACCOUNTING METHOD

Discussion

9. This Opinion is concerned with the determination of the amount of pension cost for accounting purposes. In considering the discussions and conclusions in this Opinion, it is important to keep in mind that the annual pension cost to be charged to expense ("the

provision for pension cost") is not necessarily the same as the amount to be funded for the year. The determination of the amount to be funded is a financial matter not within the purview of this Opinion.

10. The pension obligations assumed by some companies are different from those assumed by other companies. In some plans the company assumes direct responsibility for the payment of benefits described in the plan. In these cases, if the pension fund is inadequate to pay the benefits to which employees are entitled, the company is liable for the deficiency. In contrast, the terms of most funded plans limit the company's legal obligation for the payment of benefits to the amounts in the pension fund. In these cases, if the pension fund is inadequate to pay the benefits to which employees are otherwise entitled, such benefits are reduced in a manner stated in the plan and the company has no further legal obligation.

11. There is broad agreement that pension cost, including related administrative expense, should be accounted for on the accrual basis. There is not general agreement, however, about the nature of pension cost. Some view pensions solely as a form of supplemental benefit to employees in service at a particular time. Others see a broader purpose in pensions; they consider pensions to be in large part (a) a means of promoting efficiency by providing for the systematic retirement of older employees or (b) the fulfillment of a social obligation expected of business enterprises, the cost of which, as a practical matter, constitutes a business expense that must be incurred. Those who hold this second viewpoint associate pension cost, to a large extent, with the plan itself rather than with specific employees. In addition, the long-range nature of pensions causes significant uncertainties about the total amount of pension benefits ultimately to be paid and the amount of cost to be recognized. These differences in viewpoint concerning the nature of pension cost, the uncertainties regarding the amount of the estimates, and the use of many actuarial approaches, compound the difficulty in reaching agreement on the total amount of pension cost over a long period of years and on the time to recognize any particular portion applicable to an employee or group of employees. It is only natural, therefore, that different views exist concerning the preferable way to recognize pension cost. The major views are described in the following four paragraphs.

12. One view is that periodic pension cost should be provided on an actuarial basis that takes into account all estimated prospective benefit payments under a plan with respect to the existing employee

group, whether such payments relate to employee service rendered before or after the plan's adoption or amendment, and that no portion of the provision for such payments should be indefinitely deferred or treated as though, in fact, it did not exist. Those holding this view believe that the recurring omission of a portion of the provision, because of the time lag between making the provision and the subsequent benefit payments under a plan, is a failure to give accrual accounting recognition to the cost applicable to the benefits accrued over the service lives of all employees. Among those holding this view there is general agreement that cost relating to service following the adoption or amendment of a plan should be recognized ratably over the remaining service lives of employees. There is some difference of opinion, however, concerning the period of time to use in allocating that portion of the cost which the computations under some actuarial methods assign to employee service rendered before a plan's adoption or amendment. As to this cost, (a) those viewing pensions as relating solely to the existing employee group believe that it should be accounted for over the remaining service lives of those in the employ of the company at the time of the plan's adoption or amendment, whereas (b) some of those holding the broader view of pensions, referred to in Paragraph 11, believe that this cost is associated to a large extent with the plan itself and hence that the period of providing for it need not be limited to the remaining service lives of a particular group of employees but may be extended somewhat beyond that period. However, this difference of opinion relates only to the period of time over which such cost should be provided.

13. An opposing view stresses that pension cost is related to the pension benefits to be paid to the continuing employee group as a whole. Those holding this view emphasize that, in the application of accrual accounting, charges against income must be based on actual transactions and events—past, present or reasonably anticipated. They stress the long-range nature of pensions, referred to in Paragraph 11, and emphasize the uncertainties concerning the total cost of future benefits. They point out that, in the great majority of cases, provision for normal cost plus an amount equivalent to interest on unfunded prior service cost will be adequate to meet, on a continuing basis, all benefit payments under a plan. Those holding this view believe that following the view expressed in Paragraph 12 can result, over a period of years, in charging income with, and recording a balance-sheet accrual for, amounts that will not be paid as benefits.

They see no reason therefore to urge employers to provide more than normal cost plus an amount equivalent to interest on unfunded prior service cost in these circumstances, because additional amounts never expected to be paid by a going concern are not corporate costs, and thus are not appropriate charges against income. They acknowledge, however, that corporations can and do make payments to pension funds for past and prior service cost, with the result that reductions will be effected in future charges for the equivalent of interest on unfunded amounts, but they consider this to be solely a matter of financial management rather than a practice dictated by accounting considerations.

14. In many pension plans, cost recorded on the basis described in Paragraph 13 will accumulate an amount (whether funded or not) at least equal to the actuarially computed value of vested benefits (see definition of *vested benefits* in the Glossary, Appendix B). However, this result might not be achieved in some cases (for example, if the average age of the employee group is high in relation to that of expected future employee groups, or if benefits vest at a relatively early age). Some hold the view that when periodic provisions are based on normal cost plus an amount equivalent to interest such periodic provisions should be increased if they will not, within a reasonable period of time, accumulate an amount (whether funded or not) at least equal to the actuarially computed value of vested benefits. Others would require the increases in provisions only if the company has a legal obligation for the payment of such benefits.

15. Another view is that, if the company has no responsibility for paying benefits beyond the amounts in the pension fund, pension cost is discretionary and should be provided for a particular accounting period only when the company has made or has indicated its intent to make a contribution to the pension fund for the period. Others believe that pension cost is discretionary even if the company has a direct responsibility for the payment of benefits described in the plan.

Opinion

16. The Board recognizes that a company may limit its legal obligation by specifying that pensions shall be payable only to the extent of the assets in the pension fund. Experience shows, however, that with rare exceptions pension plans continue indefinitely and that termination and other limitations of the liability of the company are

not invoked while the company continues in business. Consequently, the Board believes that, in the absence of convincing evidence that the company will reduce or discontinue the benefits called for in a pension plan, the cost of the plan should be accounted for on the assumption that the company will continue to provide such benefits. This assumption implies a long-term undertaking, the cost of which should be recognized annually whether or not funded. Therefore, accounting for pension cost should not be discretionary.

17. All members of the Board believe that the entire cost of benefit payments ultimately to be made should be charged against income subsequent to the adoption or amendment of a plan and that no portion of such cost should be charged directly against retained earnings. Differences of opinion exist concerning the measure of the cost of such ultimate payments. The Board believes that the approach stated in Paragraph 12 is preferable for measuring the cost of benefit payments ultimately to be made. However, some members of the Board believe that the approach stated in Paragraph 13, in some cases with the modifications described in Paragraph 14, is more appropriate for such measurement. The Board has concluded, in the light of such differences in views and of the fact that accounting for pension cost is in a transitional stage, that the range of practices would be significantly narrowed if pension cost were accounted for at the present time within limits based on Paragraph 12, 13 and 14. Accordingly, the Board believes that the annual provision for pension cost should be based on an accounting method that uses an acceptable actuarial cost method (as defined in Paragraphs 23 and 24) and results in a provision between the minimum and maximum stated below. The accounting method and the actuarial cost method should be consistently applied from year to year.

a. *Minimum.* The annual provision for pension cost should not be less than the total of (1) normal cost, (2) an amount equivalent to interest on any unfunded prior service cost and (3) if indicated in the following sentence, a provision for vested benefits. A provision for vested benefits should be made if there is an excess of the actuarially computed value of vested benefits (see definition of *vested benefits* in the Glossary, Appendix B)[1] over the total of (1) the pension fund and (2) any balance-sheet pension accruals, less (3) any balance-sheet pension prepayments or deferred charges, at the end of the

---

[1] The actuarially computed value of vested benefits would ordinarily be based on the actuarial valuation used for the year even though such valuation would usually be as of a date other than the balance sheet date.

year, and such excess is not at least 5 percent less than the comparable excess at the beginning of the year. The provision for vested benefits should be the lesser of (A) the amount, if any, by which 5 percent of such excess at the beginning of the year is more than the amount of the reduction, if any, in such excess during the year or (B) the amount necessary to make the aggregate annual provision for pension cost equal to the total of (1) normal cost, (2) an amount equivalent to amortization, on a 40-year basis, of the past service cost (unless fully amortized), (3) amounts equivalent to amortization, on a 40-year basis, of the amounts of any increases or decreases in prior service cost arising on amendments of the plan (unless fully amortized) and (4) interest equivalents under Paragraph 42 or 43 on the difference between provisions and amounts funded.[2]

b. *Maximum.* The annual provision for pension cost should not be greater than the total of (1) normal cost, (2) 10 percent of the past service cost (until fully amortized), (3) 10 percent of the amounts of any increases or decreases in prior service cost arising on amendments of the plan (until fully amortized) and (4) interest equivalents under Paragraph 42 or 43 on the difference between provisions and amounts funded. The 10 percent limitation is considered necessary to prevent unreasonably large charges against income during a short period of years.

18. The difference between the amount which has been charged against income and the amount which has been paid should be shown in the balance sheet as accrued or prepaid pension cost. If the company has a legal obligation for pension cost in excess of amounts paid or accrued, the excess should be shown in the balance sheet as both a liability and a deferred charge. Except to the extent indicated in the preceding sentences of this paragraph, unfunded prior service cost is not a liability which should be shown in the balance sheet.

ACTUARIAL COST METHODS

Discussion

19. A number of actuarial cost methods have been developed to determine pension cost. These methods are designed primarily as funding techniques, but many of them are also useful in determining pension cost for accounting purposes. Pension cost can vary signifi-

---

[2] For purposes of this sentence, amortization should be computed as a level annual amount, including the equivalent of interest.

cantly, depending on the actuarial cost method selected; furthermore, there are many variations in the application of the methods, in the necessary actuarial assumptions concerning employee turnover, mortality, compensation levels, pension fund earnings, etc., and in the treatment of actuarial gains and losses.

20. The principal actuarial cost methods currently in use are described in Appendix A. These methods include an accrued benefit cost method and several projected benefit cost methods.

a. Under the accrued benefit cost method (unit credit method), the amount assigned to the current year usually represents the present value of the increase in present employees' retirement benefits resulting from that year's service. For an individual employee, this method results in an increasing cost from year to year because both the present value of the annual increment in benefits and the probability of reaching retirement increase as the period to retirement shortens; also, in some plans, the retirement benefits are related to salary levels, which usually increase during the years. However, the aggregate cost for a total work force of constant size tends to increase only if the average age or average compensation of the entire work force increases.

b. Under the projected benefit cost methods (entry age normal, individual level premium, aggregate and attained age normal methods), the amount assigned to the current year usually represents the level amount (or an amount based on a computed level percentage of compensation) that will provide for the estimated projected retirement benefits over the service lives of either the individual employees or the employee group, depending on the method selected. Cost computed under the projected benefit cost methods tends to be stable or to decline year by year, depending on the method selected. Cost computed under the entry age normal method is usually more stable than cost computed under any other method.

21. Some actuarial cost methods (individual level premium and aggregate methods) assign to subsequent years the cost arising at the adoption or amendment of a plan. Other methods (unit credit, entry age normal and attained age normal methods) assign a portion of the cost to years prior to the adoption or amendment of a plan, and assign the remainder to subsequent years. The portion of cost assigned to each subsequent year is called *normal cost*. At the adoption of a plan, the portion of cost assigned to prior years is called *past service cost*. At any later valuation date, the portion of cost as-

signed to prior years (which includes any remaining past service cost) is called *prior service cost*. The amount assigned as past or prior service cost and the amount assigned as normal cost vary depending on the actuarial cost method. The actuarial assignment of cost between past or prior service cost and normal cost is not indicative of the periods in which such cost should be recognized for accounting purposes.

22. In some cases, past service cost (and prior service cost arising on amendment of a plan) is funded in total; in others it is funded in part; in still others it is not funded at all. In practice, the funding of such cost is influenced by the Federal income tax laws and related regulations, which generally limit the annual deduction for such cost to 10 percent of the initial amount. There is no tax requirement that such cost be funded, but there are requirements that effectively prohibit the unfunded cost from exceeding the total of past service cost and prior service cost arising on amendment of the plan. The practical effect of the tax requirements is that on a cumulative basis normal cost plus an amount equivalent to the interest on any unfunded prior service cost must be funded. Funding of additional amounts is therefore discretionary for income tax purposes. However, neither funding nor the income tax laws and related regulations are controlling for accounting purposes.

Opinion

23. To be acceptable for determining cost for accounting purposes, an actuarial cost method should be rational and systematic and should be consistently applied so that it results in a reasonable measure of pension cost from year to year. Therefore, in applying an actuarial cost method that separately assigns a portion of cost as past or prior service cost, any amortization of such portion should be based on a rational and systematic plan and generally should result in reasonably stable annual amounts. The equivalent of interest on the unfunded portion may be stated separately or it may be included in the amortization; however, the total amount charged against income in any one year should not exceed the maximum amount described in Paragraph 17.

24. Each of the actuarial cost methods described in Appendix A, except terminal funding, is considered acceptable when the actuarial assumptions are reasonable and when the method is applied in con-

formity with the other conclusions of this Opinion. The terminal funding method is not acceptable because it does not recognize pension cost prior to retirement of employees. For the same reason, the pay-as-you-go method (which is not an actuarial cost method) is not acceptable. The acceptability of methods not discussed herein should be determined from the guidelines in this and the preceding paragraph.

ACTUARIAL GAINS AND LOSSES

Discussion

25. Actuarial assumptions necessarily are based on estimates of future events. Actual events seldom coincide with events estimated; also, as conditions change, the assumptions concerning the future may become invalid. Adjustments may be needed annually therefore to reflect actual experience, and from time to time to revise the actuarial assumptions to be used in the future. These adjustments constitute actuarial gains and losses. They may be regularly recurring (for example, minor deviations between experience and actuarial assumptions) or they may be unusual or recurring at irregular intervals (for example, substantial investment gains or losses, changes in the actuarial assumptions, plant closings, etc.).

26. In dealing with actuarial gains and losses, the primary question concerns the timing of their recognition in providing for pension cost. In practice, three methods are in use; immediate-recognition, spreading and averaging. Under the immediate-recognition method (not ordinarily used at present for net losses), net gains are applied to reduce pension cost in the year of occurrence or the following year. Under the spreading method, net gains or losses are applied to current and future cost, either through the normal cost or through the past service cost (or prior service cost on amendment). Under the averaging method, an average of annual net gains and losses, developed from those that occurred in the past with consideration of those expected to occur in the future, is applied to the normal cost.

27. The use of the immediate-recognition method sometimes results in substantial reductions in, or the complete elimination of, pension cost for one or more years. For Federal income tax purposes, when the unit credit actuarial cost method is used, and in certain other instances, actuarial gains reduce the maximum pension-cost deduction for the year of occurrence or the following year.

28. Unrealized appreciation and depreciation in the value of investments in a pension fund are forms of actuarial gains and losses. Despite short-term market fluctuations, the overall rise in the value of equity investments in recent years has resulted in the investments of pension funds generally showing net appreciation. Although appreciation is not generally recognized at present in providing for pension cost, it is sometimes recognized through the interest assumption or by introducing an assumed annual rate of appreciation as a separate actuarial assumption. In other cases, appreciation is combined with other actuarial gains and losses and applied on the immediate recognition, spreading or averaging method.

29. The amount of any unrealized appreciation to be recognized should also be considered. Some actuarial valuations recognize the full market value. Others recognize only a portion (such as 75 percent) of the market value or use a moving average (such as a five-year average) to minimize the effects of short-term market fluctuations. Another method used to minimize such fluctuations is to recognize appreciation annually based on an expected long-range growth rate (such as 3 percent) applied to the cost (adjusted for appreciation previously so recognized) of common stocks; when this method is used, the total of cost and recognized appreciation usually is not permitted to exceed a specified percentage (such as 75 percent) of the market value. Unrealized depreciation is recognized in full or on a basis similar to that used for unrealized appreciation.

Opinion

30. The Board believes that actuarial gains and losses, including realized investment gains and losses, should be given effect in the provision for pension cost in a consistent manner that reflects the long-range nature of pension cost. Accordingly, except as otherwise indicated in Paragraphs 31 and 33, actuarial gains and losses should be spread over the current year and future years or recognized on the basis of an average as described in Paragraph 26. If this is not accomplished through the routine application of the method (for example, the unit credit method—see Paragraph 27), the spreading or averaging should be accomplished by separate adjustments of the normal cost resulting from the routine application of the method. Where spreading is accomplished by separate adjustments, the Board considers a period of from 10 to 20 years to be reasonable. Alternatively, an effect similar to spreading or averaging may be obtained

by applying net actuarial gains as a reduction of prior service cost in a manner that reduces the annual amount equivalent to interest on, or the annual amount of amortization of, such prior service cost, and does not reduce the period of amortization.

31. Actuarial gains and losses should be recognized immediately if they arise from a single occurrence not directly related to the operation of the pension plan and not in the ordinary course of the employer's business. An example of such occurrences is a plant closing, in which case the actuarial gain or loss should be treated as an adjustment of the net gain or loss from that occurrence and not as an adjustment of pension cost for the year. Another example of such occurrences is a merger or acquisition accounted for as a purchase, in which case the actuarial gain or loss should be treated as an adjustment of the purchase price. However, if the transaction is accounted for as a pooling of interests, the actuarial gain or loss should generally be treated as described in Paragraph 30.

32. The Board believes unrealized appreciation and depreciation should be recognized in the determination of the provision for pension cost on a rational and systematic basis that avoids giving undue weight to short-term market fluctuations (as by using a method similar to those referred to in Paragraph 29). Such recognition should be given either in the actuarial assumptions or as described in Paragraph 30 for other actuarial gains and losses. Ordinarily appreciation and depreciation need not be recognized for debt securities expected to be held to maturity and redeemed at face value.

33. Under variable annuity and similar plans the retirement benefits vary with changes in the value of a specified portfolio of equity investments. In these cases, investment gains or losses, whether realized or unrealized, should be recognized in computing pension cost only to the extent that they will not be applied in determining retirement benefits.

EMPLOYEES INCLUDED IN COST CALCULATIONS

Discussion

34. Under some plans employees become eligible for coverage when they are employed; other plans have requirements of age or length of service or both. Some plans state only the conditions an employee must meet to receive benefits but do not otherwise deal with coverage. Ordinarily actuarial valuations exclude employees

likely to leave the company within a short time after employment. This simplifies the actuarial calculations. Accordingly, actuarial calculations ordinarily exclude employees on the basis of eligibility requirements and, in some cases, exclude covered employees during the early years of service.

35. If provisions are not made for employees from the date of employment, pension cost may be understated. On the other hand, the effect of including all employees would be partially offset by an increase in the turnover assumption; therefore, the inclusion of employees during early years of service may expand the volume of the calculations without significantly changing the provisions for pension cost.

Opinion

36. The Board believes that all employees who may reasonably be expected to receive benefits under a pension plan should be included in the cost calculations, giving appropriate recognition to anticipated turnover. As a practical matter, however, when the effect of exclusion is not material it is appropriate to omit certain employees from the calculations.

COMPANIES WITH MORE THAN ONE PLAN

Opinion

37. A company that has more than one pension plan need not use the same actuarial cost method for each one; however, the accounting for each plan should conform to this Opinion. If a company has two or more plans covering substantial portions of the same employee classes and if the assets in any of the plans ultimately can be used in paying present or future benefits of another plan or plans, such plans may be treated as one plan for purposes of determining pension cost.

DEFINED-CONTRIBUTION PLANS

Opinion

38. Some defined-contribution plans state that contributions will be made in accordance with a specified formula and that benefit pay-

ments will be based on the amounts accumulated from such contributions. For such a plan the contribution applicable to a particular year should be the pension cost for that year.

39. Some defined-contribution plans have defined benefits. In these circumstances, the plan requires careful analysis. When the substance of the plan is to provide the defined benefits, the annual pension cost should be determined in accordance with the conclusions of this Opinion applicable to defined-benefit plans.

INSURED PLANS

Opinion

40. Insured plans are forms of funding arrangements and their use should not affect the accounting principles applicable to the determination of pension cost. Cost under individual policy plans is ordinarily determined by the individual level premium method, and cost under group deferred annuity contracts is ordinarily determined by the unit credit method. Cost under deposit administration contracts, which operate similarily to trust-fund plans, may be determined on any of several methods. Some elements of pension cost, such as the application of actuarial gains (dividends, termination credits, etc.), may at times cause differences between the amounts being paid to the insurance company and the cost being recognized for accounting purposes. The Board believes that pension cost under insured plans should be determined in conformity with the conclusions of this Opinion.

41. Individual annuity or life insurance policies and group deferred annuity contracts are often used for plans covering small employee groups. Employers using one of these forms of funding exclusively do not ordinarily have ready access to actuarial advice in determining pension cost. Three factors to be considered in deciding whether the amount of net premiums paid is the appropriate charge to expense are dividends, termination credits and pension cost for employees not yet covered under the plan. Usually, the procedures adopted by insurance companies in arriving at the amount of dividends meet the requirements of Paragraph 30; consequently, in the absence of wide year-to-year fluctuations such dividends should be recognized in the year credited. Termination credits should be spread or averaged in accordance with Paragraph 30. Unless the period from date of em-

ployment to date of coverage under the plan is so long as to have a material effect on pension cost, no provision need be made for employees expected to become covered under the plan. If such a provision is made, it need not necessarily be based on the application of an actuarial cost method.

EFFECT OF FUNDING

Opinion

42. This Opinion is written primarily in terms of pension plans that are funded. The accounting described applies also to plans that are unfunded. In unfunded plans, pension cost should be determined under an acceptable actuarial cost method in the same manner as for funded plans; however, because there is no fund to earn the assumed rate of interest, the pension-cost provision for the current year should be increased by an amount equivalent to the interest that would have been earned in the current year if the prior-year provisions had been funded.

43. For funded plans, the amount of the pension cost determined under this Opinion may vary from the amount funded. When this occurs, the pension-cost provision for the year should be increased by an amount equivalent to interest on the prior-year provisions not funded or be decreased by an amount equivalent to interest on prior-year funding in excess of provisions.

44. A pension plan may become overfunded (that is, have fund assets in excess of all prior service cost assigned under the actuarial method in use for accounting purposes) as a result of contributions or as a result of actuarial gains. In determining provisions for pension cost, the effects of such overfunding are appropriately recognized in the current and future years through the operation of Paragraph 30 or 43. As to a plan that is overfunded on the effective date of this Opinion see Paragraph 48.

INCOME TAXES

Opinion

45. When pension cost is recognized for tax purposes in a period other than the one in which recognized for financial reporting, ap-

propriate consideration should be given to allocation of income taxes among accounting periods.

DISCLOSURE

Opinion

46. The Board believes that pension plans are of sufficient importance to an understanding of financial position and results of operations that the following disclosures should be made in financial statements or their notes:

1. A statement that such plans exist, identifying or describing the employee groups covered.
2. A statement of the company's accounting and funding policies.
3. The provision for pension cost for the period.
4. The excess, if any, of the actuarially computed value of vested benefits over the total of the pension fund and any balance-sheet pension accruals, less any pension prepayments or deferred charges.
5. Nature and effect of significant matters affecting comparability for all periods presented, such as changes in accounting methods (actuarial cost method, amortization of past and prior service cost, treatment of actuarial gains and losses, etc.), changes in circumstances (actuarial assumptions, etc.), or adoption or amendment of a plan.

An example of what the Board considers to be appropriate disclosure is as follows:

> The company and its subsidiaries have several pension plans covering substantially all of their employees, including certain employees in foreign countries. The total pension expense for the year was $............, which includes, as to certain of the plans, amortization of prior service cost over periods ranging from 25 to 40 years. The company's policy is to fund pension cost accrued. The actuarially computed value of vested benefits for all plans as of December 31, 19...., exceeded the total of the pension fund and balance-sheet accruals less pension prepayments and deferred charges by approximately $............. A change during the year in the actuarial cost method used in computing pension cost had the effect of reducing net income for the year by approximately $...............

CHANGES IN ACCOUNTING METHOD

Opinion

47. On occasion a company may change its method of accounting for pension cost from one acceptable method under this Opinion to another. Such a change might be a change in the actuarial cost method, in the amortization of past and prior service cost, in the treatment of actuarial gains and losses, or in other factors. When such a change is made subsequent to the effective date of this Opinion, a question arises about the accounting for the difference between the cost actually provided under the old method and the cost that would have been provided under the new method. The Board believes that pension cost provided under an acceptable method of accounting in prior periods should not be changed subsequently. Therefore, the effect on prior-year cost of a change in accounting method should be applied prospectively to the cost of the current year and future years, in a manner consistent with the conclusions of this Opinion, and not retroactively as an adjustment of retained earnings or otherwise. The change and its effect should be disclosed as indicated in Paragraph 46.

TRANSITION TO RECOMMENDED PRACTICES

Opinion

48. For purposes of this Opinion, any unamortized prior service cost (computed under the actuarial cost method to be used for accounting purposes in the future) on the effective date of this Opinion may be treated as though it arose from an amendment of the plan on that date rather than on the actual dates of adoption or amendment of the plan. If the pension plan is overfunded (see Paragraph 44) on the effective date of this Opinion, the amount by which it is overfunded (computed under the actuarial cost method to be used for accounting purposes in the future) should be treated as an actuarial gain realized on that date and should be accounted for as described in Paragraph 30.

49. The effect of any changes in accounting methods made as a result of the issuance of this Opinion should be applied prospectively to the cost of the current year and future years in a manner consistent with the conclusions of this Opinion, and not retroactively

by an adjustment of retained earnings or otherwise. The change and its effect should be disclosed as indicated in Paragraph 46.

EFFECTIVE DATE

50. This Opinion shall be effective for fiscal periods beginning after December 31, 1966. However, where feasible the Board urges earlier compliance with this Opinion.[3]

NOTES

Opinions present the considered opinion of at least two-thirds of the members of the Accounting Principles Board, reached on a formal vote after examination of the subject matter.

Except as indicated in the succeeding paragraph, the authority of the Opinions rests upon their general acceptability. While it is recognized that general rules may be subject to exception, the burden of justifying departures from Board Opinions must be assumed by those who adopt other practices.

Action of Council of the Institute (Special Bulletin, Disclosure of Departures From Opinions of Accounting Principles Board, *October 1964) provides that:*

  a. *"Generally accepted accounting principles" are those principles which have substantial authoritative support.*
  b. *Opinions of the Accounting Principles Board constitute "substantial authoritative support."*
  c. *"Substantial authoritative support" can exist for accounting principles that differ from Opinions of the Accounting Principles Board.*

The Council action also requires that departures from Board Opinions be disclosed in footnotes to the financial statements or in independent auditors' reports when the effect of the departure on the financial statements is material.

Unless otherwise stated, Opinions of the Board are not intended to be retroactive. They are not intended to be applicable to immaterial items.

---

[3] The Opinion entitled "Accounting for the Cost of Pension Plans" was adopted unanimously by the 20 members of the Board.

Accounting Principles Board (1966–1967)

APPENDIX A: ACTUARIAL VALUATIONS, ASSUMPTIONS AND COST METHODS

Actuarial Valuations

An actuarial valuation of a pension plan is the process used by actuaries for determining the amounts an employer is to contribute (pay, fund) under a pension plan (except where an insured arrangement calls for payment of specified premiums). A valuation is made as of a specific date, which need not coincide with the end of the period for which a payment based on the valuation will be made. Indeed, it is uncommon for such a coincidence of dates to exist. Among other factors, a time lag is necessary in order to compile the data and to permit the actuary to make the necessary calculations. Although annual valuations are, perhaps, the rule, some employers have valuations made at less frequent intervals, in some cases as infrequently as every five years. The calculations are made for a closed group—ordinarily, employees presently covered by the plan, former employees having vested rights and retired employees currently receiving benefits.

An initial step in making a valuation is to determine the present value on the valuation date of benefits to be paid over varying periods of time in the future to employees after retirement (plus any

---

Note: For further discussion see Appendix C of Accounting Research Study No. 8, *Accounting for the Cost of Pension Plans* by Ernest L. Hicks, CPA, published by the American Institute of Certified Public Accountants in 1965.

other benefits under the plan). An actuarial cost method (see description in a later section of this Appendix) is then applied to this present value to determine the contributions to be made by the employer.

The resulting determinations are estimates, since in making a valuation a number of significant uncertainties concerning future events must be resolved by making several actuarial assumptions.

Actuarial Assumptions

The uncertainties in estimating the cost of a pension plan relate to (1) interest (return on funds invested), (2) expenses of administration and (3) the amounts and timing of benefits to be paid with respect to presently retired employees, former employees whose benefits have vested and present employees.

Interest (Return on Funds Invested). The rate of interest used in an actuarial valuation is an expression of the average rate of earnings that can be expected on the funds invested or to be invested to provide for the future benefits. Since in most instances the investments include equity securities as well as debt securities, the earnings include dividends as well as interest; gains and losses on investments are also a factor. For simplicity, however, the rate is ordinarily called the interest rate.

Expenses of Administration. In many instances the expenses of administering a pension plan—for example, fees of attorneys, actuaries and trustees, and the cost of keeping pension records—are borne directly by the employer. In other cases, such expenses, or some of them, are paid by a trust or insurance company from funds contributed by the employer. In the latter cases, expenses to be incurred in the future must be estimated in computing the employer's pension cost.

Benefits. Several assumptions must be made as to the amounts and timing of the future benefits whose present value is used in expressing the cost of a pension plan. The principal assumptions are as follows:

a. Future Compensation Levels. Benefits under some pension plans depend in part on future compensation levels. Under plans of this type, an estimate is ordinarily made of normal increases expected from the progression of employees through the various earnings-rate categories, based on the employer's experience. General earnings-level increases, such as those which may result from inflation, are usually excluded from this actuarial assumption.

b. Cost-of-Living. To protect the purchasing power of retirement benefits, some plans provide that the benefits otherwise determined will be adjusted from time to time to reflect variations in a specific index, such as the Consumer Price Index of the United States Bureau of Labor Statistics. In estimating the cost of such a plan, expected future changes in the cost-of-living index may be included in the actuarial assumptions.

c. Mortality. The length of time an employee covered by a pension plan will live is an important factor in estimating the cost of the benefit payments he will receive. If an employee dies before he becomes eligible for pension benefits, he receives no payments, although in some plans his beneficiaries receive lump-sum or periodic benefits. The total amount of pension benefits for employees who reach retirement is determined in large part by how long they live thereafter. Estimates regarding mortality are based on mortality tables.

d. Retirement Age. Most plans provide a normal retirement age, but many plans permit employees to work thereafter under certain conditions. Some plans provide for retirement in advance of the normal age in case of disability, and most plans permit early retirement at the employee's option under certain conditions. When there are such provisions, an estimate is made of their effect on the amount and timing of the benefits which will ultimately be paid.

e. Turnover. In many plans, some employees who leave employment with the employer before completing vesting requirements forfeit their rights to receive benefits. In estimating the amount of future benefits, an allowance for the effect of turnover may be made.

f. Vesting. Many plans provide that after a stated number of years of service an employee becomes entitled to receive benefits (commencing at his normal retirement age and usually varying in amount with his number of years of service) even though he leaves the company for a reason other than retirement. This is taken into consideration in estimating the effect of turnover.

g. Social Security Benefits. For plans providing for a reduction of pensions by all or part of social security benefits, it is necessary in estimating future pension benefits to estimate the effect of future social security benefits. Ordinarily, this estimate is based on the assumption that such benefits will remain at the level in effect at the time the valuation is being made.

Actuarial Gains and Losses. The likelihood that actual events will coincide with each of the assumptions used is so remote as to constitute an impossibility. As a result, the actuarial assumptions used may be changed from time to time as experience and judgment dictate. In addition, whether or not the assumptions as to events in the future are changed, it is often necessary to recognize in the calculations the effect of differences between actual prior experience and the assumptions used in the past.

Actuarial Cost Methods

Actuarial cost methods have been developed by actuaries as funding techniques to be used in actuarial valuations. As indicated in Paragraph 19 of the accompanying Opinion, many of the actuarial cost methods are also useful for accounting purposes. The following discussion of the principal methods describes them as funding techniques (to simplify the discussion, references to prior service cost arising on amendment of a plan have been omitted; such cost would ordinarily be treated in a manner consistent with that described for past service cost). Their application for accounting purposes is described in the accompanying Opinion.

Accrued Benefit Cost Method—Unit Credit Method. Under the unit credit method, future service benefits (pension benefits based on service after the inception of a plan) are funded as they accrue—that is, as each employee works out the service period involved. Thus, the normal cost under this method for a particular year is the present value of the units of future benefit credited to employees for service in that year (hence unit credit). For example, if a plan provides benefits of $5 per month for each year of credited service, the normal cost for a particular employee for a particular year is the present value (adjusted for mortality and usually for turnover) of an annuity of $5 per month beginning at the employee's anticipated retirement date and continuing throughout his life.

The past service cost under the unit credit method is the present value at the plan's inception date of the units of future benefit credited to employees for service prior to the inception date.

The annual contribution under the unit credit method ordinarily comprises (1) the normal cost and (2) an amount for past service cost. The latter may comprise only an amount equivalent to interest on the unfunded balance or may also include an amount intended to reduce the unfunded balance.

As to an individual employee, the annual normal cost for an equal unit of benefit each year increases because the period to the employee's retirement continually shortens and the probability of reaching retirement increases; also, in some plans, the retirement benefits are related to salary levels, which usually increase during the years. As to the employees collectively, however, the step-up effect is masked, since older employees generating the highest annual cost are continually replaced by new employees generating the lowest. For a mature employee group, the normal cost would tend to be the same each year.

The unit credit method is almost always used when the funding instrument is a group annuity contract and may also be used in trusteed plans and deposit administration contracts where the benefit is a stated amount per year of service. This method is not frequently used where the benefit is a fixed amount (for example, $100 per month) or where the current year's benefit is based on earnings of a future period.

Projected Benefit Cost Methods. As explained above, the accrued benefit cost method (unit credit method) recognizes the cost of benefits only when they have accrued (in the limited sense that the employee service on which benefits are based has been rendered). By contrast, the projected benefit cost methods look forward. That is, they assign the entire cost of an employee's *projected* benefits to past, present and future periods. This is done in a manner not directly related to the periods during which the service on which the benefits are based has been or will be rendered. The principal projected benefit cost methods are discussed below.

a. Entry Age Normal Method. Under the entry age normal method, the normal costs are computed on the assumption (1) that every employee entered the plan (thus, entry age) at the time of employment or at the earliest time he would have been eligible if the plan had been in existence and (2) that contributions have been made on this basis from the entry age to the date of the actuarial valuation. The contributions are the level annual amounts which, if accumulated at the rate of interest used in the actuarial valuation, would result in a fund equal to the present value of the pensions at retirement for the employees who survive to that time.

Normal cost under this method is the level amount to be contributed for each year. When a plan is established after the company has been in existence for some time, past service cost under this method at the plan's inception date is theoretically the amount of the fund that would have been accumulated had annual contributions equal to the normal cost been made in prior years.

In theory, the entry age normal method is applied on an individual basis. It may be applied, however, on an aggregate basis, in which case separate amounts are not determined for individual employees. Further variations in practice often encountered are (1) the use of an average entry age, (2) the use, particularly when benefits are based on employees' earnings, of a level percentage of payroll in determining annual payments and (3) the computation of past service cost as the difference between the present value of employees' projected benefits and the present value of the employer's projected normal cost contributions. In some plans, the normal cost contribution rate may be based on a stated amount per employee. In other plans the normal cost contribution itself may be stated as a flat amount.

In valuations for years other than the initial year the past service cost may be frozen (that is, the unfunded amount of such cost is changed only to recognize payments and the effect of interest). Accordingly, actuarial gains and losses are spread into the future, entering into the normal cost for future years. If past service cost is not frozen, the unfunded amount includes the effects of actuarial gains and losses realized prior to the date of the valuation being made.

The annual contribution under the entry age normal method ordinarily comprises (1) the normal cost and (2) an amount for past service cost. The latter may comprise only an amount equivalent to interest on the unfunded balance or may also include an amount intended to reduce the unfunded balance.

The entry age normal method is often used with trusteed plans and deposit administration contracts.

b. *Individual Level Premium Method.* The individual level premium method assigns the cost of each employee's pension in level annual amounts, or as a level percentage of the employee's compensation, over the period from the inception date of a plan (or the date of his entry into the plan, if later) to his retirement date. Thus, past service cost is not determined separately but is included in normal cost.

The most common use of the individual level premium method is with funding by individual insurance or annuity policies. It may be

used, however, with trusteed plans and deposit administration contracts.

In plans using individual annuity policies, the employer is pro-
tected against actuarial losses, since premiums paid are not ordinarily
subject to retroactive increases. The insurance company may, however, pass part of any actuarial gains along to the employer by means
of dividends. Employee turnover may be another source of actuarial
gains under such insured plans, since all or part of the cash surrender
values of policies previously purchased for employees leaving the employer for reasons other than retirement may revert to the company
(or to the trust). Dividends and cash surrender values are ordinarily
used to reduce the premiums payable for the next period.

The individual level premium method generates annual costs
which are initially very high and which ultimately drop to the level
of the normal cost determined under the entry age normal method.
The high initial costs arise because the past service cost (although
not separately identified) for employees near retirement when the
plan is adopted is in effect amortized over a very short period.

c. *Aggregate Method.* The aggregate method applies on a collective basis the principle followed for individuals in the individual
level premium method. That is, the entire unfunded cost of future
pension benefits (including benefits to be paid to employees who
have retired as of the date of the valuation) is spread over the average
future service lives of employees who are active as of the date of the
valuation. In most cases this is done by the use of a percentage of
payroll.

The aggregate method does not deal separately with past service
cost (but includes such cost in normal cost). Actuarial gains and
losses enter into the determination of the contribution rate and, consequently, are spread over future periods.

Annual contributions under the aggregate method decrease, but
the rate of decrease is less extreme than under the individual level
premium method. The aggregate cost method amortizes past service
cost (not separately identified) over the average future service lives
of employees, thus avoiding the very short individual amortization
periods of the individual level premium method.

The aggregate method may be modified by introducing past service
cost. If the past service cost is determined by the entry age normal
method, the modified aggregate method is the same as the entry age
normal method applied on the aggregate basis. If the past service

cost is determined by the unit credit method, the modified aggregate method is called the attained age normal method (discussed below).

The aggregate method is used principally with trusteed plans and deposit administration contracts.

d. Attained Age Normal Method. The attained age normal method is a variant of the aggregate method or individual level premium method in which past service cost, determined under the unit credit method, is recognized separately. The cost of each employee's benefits assigned to years after the inception of the plan is spread over the employee's future service life. Normal cost contributions under the attained age normal method, usually determined as a percentage of payroll, tend to decline but less markedly than under the aggregate method or the individual level premium method.

As with the unit credit and entry age normal methods, the annual contribution for past service cost may comprise only an amount equivalent to interest on the unfunded balance or may also include an amount intended to reduce the unfunded balance.

The attained age normal method is used with trusteed plans and deposit administration contracts.

Terminal Funding. Under terminal funding, funding for future benefit payments is made only at the end of an employee's period of active service. At that time the employer either purchases a single-premium annuity which will provide the retirement benefit or makes an actuarially equivalent contribution to a trust. (Note—This method is not acceptable for determining the provision for pension cost under the accompanying Opinion.)

APPENDIX B: GLOSSARY

Accrue (Accrual). When *accrue (accrual)* is used in accounting discussions in the accompanying Opinion, it has the customary accounting meaning. When used in relation to actuarial terms or procedures, however, the intended meaning differs somewhat. When actuaries say that pension benefits, actuarial costs or actuarial liabilities have *accrued,* they ordinarily mean that the amounts are associated, either specifically or by a process of allocation, with years of employee service before the date of a particular valuation of a pension plan. Actuaries do not ordinarily intend their use of the word *accrue* to have the more conclusive accounting significance.

Accrued Benefit Cost Method. An *actuarial cost method*. See Appendix A.

Actuarial Assumptions. Factors which actuaries use in tentatively resolving uncertainties concerning future events affecting pension cost; for example, mortality rate, employee turnover, compensation levels, investment earnings, etc. See Appendix A.

Actuarial Cost Method. A particular technique used by actuaries for establishing the amount and incidence of the annual actuarial cost of pension plan benefits, or benefits and expenses, and the related actuarial liability. Sometimes called *funding method*. See Appendix A.

Actuarial Gains (Losses). The effects on actuarially calculated pension cost of (*a*) deviations between actual prior experience and the actuarial assumptions used or (*b*) changes in actuarial assumptions as to future events.

Actuarial Liability. The excess of the present value, as of the date of a pension plan valuation, of prospective pension benefits and administrative expenses over the sum of (1) the amount in the pension fund and (2) the present value of future contributions for normal cost determined by any of several actuarial cost methods. (Sometimes referred to as *unfunded actuarial liability*.)

Actuarial Valuation. The process by which an actuary estimates the present value of benefits to be paid under a pension plan and calculates the amounts of employer contributions or accounting charges for pension cost. See Appendix A.

Actuarially Computed Value. See *present value*.

Actuarially Computed Value of Vested Benefits. See *vested benefits*.

Actuary. There are no statutory qualifications required for actuaries. Membership in the American Academy of Actuaries, a comprehensive organization of the profession in the United States, is generally considered to be acceptable evidence of professional qualification.

Aggregate Method. An *actuarial cost method*. See Appendix A.

Assumptions. See *actuarial assumptions*.

Attained Age Normal Method. An *actuarial cost method*. See Appendix A.

Benefits (Pension Benefits) (Retirement Benefits). The pensions and any other payments to which employees or their beneficiaries may be entitled under a pension plan.

Contribute (Contribution). When used in connection with a pension plan, *contribute* ordinarily is synonymous with pay.

Deferred Compensation Plan. An arrangement whereby specified portions of the employee's compensation are payable in the form of retirement benefits.

Deferred Profit-Sharing Plan. An arrangement whereby an employer provides for future retirement benefits for employees from specified portions of the earnings of the business; the benefits for each employee are usually the amounts which can be provided by accumulated amounts specifically allocated to him.

Defined-Benefit Plan. A pension plan stating the benefits to be received by employees after retirement, or the method of determining such benefits. The employer's contributions under such a plan are determined actuarially on the basis of the benefits expected to become payable.

Defined-Contribution Plan. A pension plan which (*a*) states the benefits to be received by employees after retirement or the method of determining such benefits (as in the case of a defined-benefit plan) and (*b*) accompanies a separate agreement that provides a formula for calculating the employer's contributions (for example, a fixed amount for each ton produced or for each hour worked, or a fixed percentage of compensation). Initially, the benefits stated in the plan are those which the contributions expected to be made by the employer can provide. If later the contributions are found to be inadequate or excessive for the purpose of funding the stated benefits on the basis originally contemplated, either the contributions or the benefits, or both, may be subsequently adjusted. In one type of defined-contribution plan (money-purchase plan) the employer's contributions are determined for, and allocated with respect to, specific individuals, usually as a percentage of compensation; the benefits for each employee are the amounts which can be provided by the sums contributed for him.

Deposit Administration Contract. A funding instrument provided by an insurance company under which amounts contributed by an employer are not identified with specific employees until they retire. When an employee retires, the insurance company issues an annuity which will provide the benefits stipulated in the pension plan and transfers the single premium for the annuity from the employer's accumulated contributions.

Entry Age Normal Method. An *actuarial cost method*. See Appendix A.

Fund. Used as a verb, *fund* means to pay over to a funding agency. Used as a noun, *fund* refers to assets accumulated in the hands of a funding agency for the purpose of meeting retirement benefits when they become due.

Funded. The portion of pension cost that has been paid to a funding agency is said to have been *funded*.

Funding Agency. An organization or individual, such as a specific corporate or individual trustee or an insurance company, which provides facilities for the accumulation of assets to be used for the payment of benefits under a pension plan; an organization, such as a specific life insurance company, which provides facilities for the purchase of such benefits.

Funding Method. See *actuarial cost method*.

Individual Level Premium Method. An *actuarial cost method*. See Appendix A.

Interest. The return earned or to be earned on funds invested or to be invested to provide for future pension benefits. In calling the return *interest*, it is recognized that in addition to interest on debt securities the earnings of a pension fund may include dividends on equity securities, rentals on real estate, and realized and unrealized gains or (as offsets) losses on fund investments. See Appendix A.

Mortality Rate. Death rate—the proportion of the number of deaths in a specified group to the number living at the beginning of the period in which the deaths occur. Actuaries use mortality tables, which show death rates for each age, in estimating the amount of future retirement benefits which will become payable. See Appendix A.

Normal Cost. The annual cost assigned, under the actuarial cost method in use, to years subsequent to the inception of a pension plan or to a particular valuation date. See *past service cost, prior service cost*.

Past Service Cost. Pension cost assigned, under the actuarial cost method in use, to years prior to the inception of a pension plan. See *normal cost, prior service cost*.

Pay-As-You-Go. A method of recognizing pension cost only when benefits are paid to retired employees. (Note—This is not an acceptable method for accounting purposes under the accompanying Opinion.)

Pension Fund. See *fund.*

Present Value (Actuarially Computed Value). The current worth of an amount or series of amounts payable or receivable in the future. *Present value* is determined by discounting the future amount or amounts at a predetermined rate of interest. In pension plan valuations, actuaries often combine arithmetic factors representing probability (e.g., mortality, withdrawal, future compensation levels) with arithmetic factors representing discount (interest). Consequently, to actuaries, determining the present value of future pension benefits may mean applying factors of both types.

Prior Service Cost. Pension cost assigned, under the actuarial cost method in use, to years prior to the date of a particular actuarial valuation. *Prior service cost* includes any remaining past service cost. See *normal cost, past service cost.*

Projected Benefit Cost Method. A type of *actuarial cost method.* See Appendix A.

Provision (Provide). An accounting term meaning a charge against income for an estimated expense, such as pension cost.

Service. Employment taken into consideration under a pension plan. Years of employment before the inception of a plan constitute an employee's past service; years thereafter are classified in relation to the particular actuarial valuation being made or discussed. Years of employment (including past service) prior to the date of a particular valuation constitute prior service; years of employment following the date of the valuation constitute future service.

Terminal Funding. An *actuarial cost method.* See Appendix A. (Note—This is not an acceptable *actuarial cost method* for accounting purposes under the accompanying Opinion.)

Trust Fund Plan. A pension plan for which the funding instrument is a trust agreement.

Turnover. Termination of employment for a reason other than death or retirement. See *withdrawal,* Appendix A.

Unit Credit Method. An *actuarial cost method.* See Appendix A.

Valuation. See *actuarial valuation,* Appendix A.

Vested Benefits. Benefits that are not contingent on the employee's continuing in the service of the employer. In some plans the payment of the benefits will begin only when the employee reaches the normal retirement date; in other plans the payment of the benefits will begin when the employee retires (which may be before or after the normal retirement date). The *actuarially computed value of vested benefits,* as used in this Opinion, represents the present value, at the date of determination, of the sum of (*a*) the benefits expected to become payable to former employees who have retired, or who have terminated service with vested rights, at the date of determination; and (*b*) the benefits, based on service rendered prior to the date of determination, expected to become payable at future dates to present employees, taking into account the probable time that employees will retire, at the vesting percentages applicable at the date of determination. The determination of vested benefits is not affected by other conditions, such as inadequacy of the pension fund, which may prevent the employee from receiving the vested benefits.

Withdrawal. The removal of an employee from coverage under a pension plan for a reason other than death or retirement. See *turnover.*

FASB Interpretation No. 3

Accounting for the Cost of Pension Plans Subject to the Employee Retirement Income Security Act of 1974

INTRODUCTION

1. The Employee Retirement Income Security Act of 1974 (commonly referred to as the Pension Reform Act) became law on September 2, 1974. It is principally concerned with the funding of pension plans, the conditions for employee participation and for vesting of benefits, and the safeguarding of employees' pension rights. Pension plans adopted after January 1, 1974 are subject to the participation, vesting, and funding requirements of the Act for plan years beginning after September 2, 1974. Pension plans in existence on January 1, 1974 are not subject to those requirements until plan years beginning after December 31, 1975, unless earlier compliance is elected.

2. The Financial Accounting Standards Board has analyzed the Act to determine whether there is a need to reconsider *APB Opinion No. 8*, "Accounting for the Cost of Pension Plans." As a result of that analysis, the Board has placed the overall subject of pension accounting, including accounting and reporting by pension trusts, on its technical agenda. Pending completion of that project, the

An interpretation of *APB Opinion No. 8*, Financial Accounting Standards Board, Stamford, Connecticut, December 1974. Copyright © by the Financial Accounting Standards Board, High Ridge Park, Stamford, Conn. 06905. Reprinted with permission. Copies of the complete document are available from the FASB.

Board is issuing this Interpretation to clarify the accounting for the cost of pension plans covered by the Act.

INTERPRETATION

3. A fundamental concept of APB *Opinion No. 8* is that the annual pension cost to be charged to expense for financial accounting purposes is not necessarily determined by the funding of a pension plan. Therefore, no change in the minimum and maximum limits for the annual provision for pension cost set forth in paragraph 17 of APB *Opinion No. 8* is required as a result of the Act. Compliance with the Act's participation, vesting, or funding requirements may result, however, in a change in the amount of pension cost to be charged to expense periodically for financial accounting purposes even though no change in accounting methods is made. Paragraph 17 of APB *Opinion No. 8* requires that "the entire cost of benefit payments ultimately to be made should be charged against income subsequent to the adoption or amendment of a plan." Consistent with that requirement and within the minimum and maximum limits of paragraph 17 of APB *Opinion No. 8*, any change in pension cost resulting from compliance with the Act shall enter into the determination of periodic provisions for pension expense *subsequent* to the date a plan becomes subject to the Act's participation, vesting, and funding requirements. That date will be determined either by the effective dates prescribed by the Act or by an election of earlier compliance with the requirements of the Act.

4. If, *prior* to the date a plan becomes subject to the Act's participation, vesting, and funding requirements, it appears likely that compliance will have a significant effect in the future on the amount of an enterprise's (*a*) periodic provision for pension expense, (*b*) periodic funding of pension costs, or (*c*) unfunded vested benefits, this fact and an estimate of the effect shall be disclosed in the notes to the financial statements.[1]

5. Based on an analysis of information presently available, the Board does not believe that the Act creates a legal obligation for unfunded pension costs that warrants accounting recognition as a

---

[1] The Board recognizes that actuarial computations or other information may not be available in time to permit disclosure of an estimate of the effect in notes to financial statements for fiscal periods ending in 1974 or early in 1975. If an estimate cannot be furnished, an explanation shall be provided.

liability pursuant to paragraph 18 of *APB Opinion No. 8* except in the following two respects. First, an enterprise with a plan subject to the Act must fund a minimum amount annually unless a waiver is obtained from the Secretary of the Treasury. If a waiver is not obtained, the amount currently required to be funded shall be recognized as a liability by a charge to pension expense for the period, by a deferred charge, or by a combination of both, whatever is appropriate under *APB Opinion No. 8*. Second, in the event of the termination of a pension plan, the Act imposes a liability on an enterprise. When there is convincing evidence that a pension plan will be terminated, evidenced perhaps by a formal commitment by management to terminate the plan, and the liability on termination will exceed fund assets and related prior accruals, the excess liability shall be accrued. If the amount of the excess liability cannot be reasonably determined, disclosure of the circumstances shall be made in the notes to the financial statements, including an estimate of the possible range of the liability.

EFFECTIVE DATE

6. This Interpretation shall be effective on December 31, 1974.

This Interpretation was adopted by the unanimous vote of the seven members of the Financial Accounting Standards Board following submission to the members of the Financial Accounting Standards Advisory Council.

> Marshall S. Armstrong, *Chairman*
> Donald J. Kirk
> Arthur L. Litke
> Robert E. Mays
> John W. Queenan
> Walter Schuetze
> Robert T. Sprouse

Selected Bibliography

American Institute of Certified Public Accountants, "Accounting for the Cost of Pension Plans," *APB Opinion No. 8* (New York, 1966).

American Institute of Certified Public Accountants, "Accounting for the Cost of Pension Plans," *ARB No. 47* (New York, 1956).

American Institute of Certified Public Accountants, "Audits of Voluntary Health and Welfare Organizations," *Industry Audit Guide,* (New York, 1974).

American Institute of Certified Public Accountants, "Report of the Study on Establishment of Accounting Principles," *Establishing Financial Accounting Standards* (New York, March 1972).

American Institute of Certified Public Accountants, "Report of the Study Group on the Objectives of Financial Statements," *Objectives of Financial Statements* (New York, October 1973).

Arthur Andersen & Co., *Objectives of Financial Statements for Business Enterprises* (Chicago, 1972).

Arthur Andersen & Co., *Accounting Standards for Business Enterprises Throughout the World* (Chicago, 1974).

Bankers Trust Company, "1975 Study of Corporate Pension Plans," (New York, 1975).

Bassett, Preston C., "Who What and When of Accounting and Reporting for Pension Plans," *Financial Executive,* vol. XLIV, no. 1 (January 1976).

Blackstock, Henry T., *Portfolio Comments: Higher Pension Costs Ahead* (New York: Goldman, Sachs & Co., December 1974).

Chase Manhattan Bank, "Survey 2 on Pension Fund Financing" (New York, 1972).

Cramer, Joe J., Jr., and Schrader, William J., "Elements of 'Pension Costs,'" *The Journal of Risk and Insurance,* vol. 35, no. 2 (June 1968).

Cramer, Joe J., Jr., and Neyhart, Charles A., "Accounting for Pensions: A Contemporary Perspective," *Financial Executive,* vol. XLIV, no. 1 (January 1976).

Deaton, William D., and Weygandt, Jerry J., "Disclosures Related to Pension Plans," *The Journal of Accountancy,* vol. 139, no. 1, (January 1975).

Dewhirst, John F., "A Conceptual Approach to Pension Accounting," *The Accounting Review,* vol. 46, no. 2 (April 1971).

Dreher, William A., "Alternatives Available under APB Opinion No. 8: An Actuary's View," *The Journal of Accountancy,* vol. 124, no. 3, (September 1967).

Financial Accounting Standards Board, "An Analysis of Issues Related to Accounting and Reporting for Employee Benefit Plans," *Discussion Memorandum* (Stamford, Conn., 1975).

Financial Accounting Standards Board, "Accounting for the Cost of Pension Plans Subject to the Employee Retirement Income Security Act of 1974," *Interpretation No. 3,* (Stamford, Conn., 1974).

Hershman, Arlene, "The Big Pension Fund Drain," *Dun's Review,* vol. 106, no. 1 (July 1975).

Hicks, Ernest L., "Accounting for the Cost of Pension Plans," *Accounting Research Study No. 8* (New York: American Institute of Certified Public Accountants, 1965).

Jackson, Paul H., "Inflation, Interest Rates, and Salary Increases," *The Proceedings of the Conference of Actuaries in Public Practice,* vol. XXIV (1974-1975).

McGill, Dan M., and Winklevoss, Howard E., "A Quantitative Analysis of Actuarial Cost Methods for Pension Plans," *The Proceedings of the Conference of Actuaries in Public Practice,* vol. XXIII (1973-1974).

McGill, Dan M., *Fundamentals of Private Pensions,* 3d ed. (Homewood, Ill.: Richard D. Irwin, Inc., 1975).

Ogden, Warde B., "Survey of 260 Pension Plans Reveals Wide Variety of Accounting for Costs, Plus Some Hazards," *The Journal of Accountancy,* vol. 93, no. 1 (January 1952).

Pomeranz, Felix; Ramsey, Gordon P.; and Steinberg, Richard M., *Pensions, An Accounting and Management Guide* (New York: The Ronald Press, 1975).

Trowbridge, C. L., "Fundamentals of Pension Funding," *Transactions of the Society of Actuaries*, 1952, vol. 4.

Trowbridge, C. L., and Farr, C. E., *The Theory and Practice of Pension Funding* (Homewood, Ill.: Richard D. Irwin, Inc., 1976).

Winklevoss, Howard E., *Pension Mathematics: With Numerical Illustrations* (Homewood, Ill.: Richard D. Irwin, Inc., 1977).